Alaskan
HISTORY – IN BRIEF

By James K. Barnett

Library of Congress Control Number: 2011921216

ISBN: 978-1-57833-517-6

First Printing February, 2011

Printed by Everbest Printing Co., Ltd., Nansha, China, through Alaska Print Brokers, Anchorage, Alaska.

Cover design & layout:
Vered R. Mares, Todd Communications

Editors: Liz Russo, Eloise Robbins, Flip Todd

Cover Art:
Mt. McKinley (1920) by Sydney Laurence
Oil on Canvas (10" x 8") used by permission from
Len Braarud of Braarud Fine Art, La Conner, WA.

This book was typeset in 10 point Adobe Caslon Pro.

Additional copies of this book may be purchased from the publisher for $16.95 (including $4 First Class mail) *inside* U.S. and $22.95 (including $10 First Class mail) *outside* U.S.

Published by
Todd Communications
611 E. 12th Ave., Suite 102
Anchorage, Alaska 99501-4603
(907) 274-TODD (8633) • Fax: (907) 929-5550
with other offices in Ketchikan, Juneau, Fairbanks and Nome Alaska

sales@toddcom.com • WWW.ALASKABOOKSANDCALENDARS.COM

Alaskan
HISTORY – IN BRIEF
By James K. Barnett

Table of Contents

Preface

The history of Alaska is a complex and fascinating tale of the many tough and talented residents who have called the Far North home for millennia. This is the story, or an accumulation of many stories, about the people who contributed to the settlement, growth and realization of the Alaskan dream. It is a well-known adage that "Those who cannot remember the past are condemned to repeat it." Today Alaskans and visitors study and reflect on this unique history to learn from the experiences of the past and contemplate challenges for the future.

Alaska is a place for modern pioneers filled with the romance and ideals embodied in the Last Frontier. Resource extraction and the boom and bust cycles that permeate Alaska's history still dominate the state. But now citizens and politicians debate how new mining, drilling and pipeline projects will impact the environment. Further, Alaskans consider the implications of global warming, whether or not caused or exacerbated by human activity, as Alaska is the bellwether of the impacts from climate change.

In 1961, British historian E. H. Carr wrote, "History begins with the handing down of tradition; and tradition means the carrying of the habits and lessons of the past into the future. Records of the past begin to be kept for the benefit of future generations." The difficulty in writing this condensed history is to place the emphasis on the contributions and calamities of these many individuals in a succinct fashion to lead the reader to a better understanding of the lessons and accomplishments of the past.

This volume is dedicated to the early Alaskans who made their mark on the state and its history, as well as the leaders who contemplate that history in charting its future. The 49th state's complex history, immense wealth and wilderness values will ensure that decisions will no doubt eventually flow down some pipeline or river valley to benefit Alaskans and Americans alike.

I am especially indebted to Flip Todd, owner of Todd Communications, for conceiving this project and my wife, Marilyn Barnett, who read every word of the manuscript several times and offered priceless support on its flow and content. In addition, Judy Bittner (Alaska State Historic Preservation Officer), Darrell Lewis (National Park Service), Brian Meacham (archivist with the Academy of Motion Picture Arts and Sciences), Tom Meacham (Anchorage attorney), Paul Peyton (fisheries consultant), Malcolm Roberts (Anchorage businessman) and John Reeder (Anchorage attorney) for their contributions to chapters within their special expertise. Their considerable knowledge of Alaska history and current issues was invaluable for the preparation of this publication.

– James K. Barnett
Anchorage, Alaska

About the Author

James K. Barnett has been an Alaska attorney in private practice in Anchorage since 1974. He is both a former deputy commissioner of the Alaska Department of Natural Resources and was an elected member of the Anchorage Municipal Assembly. He is also the long-time president of the Cook Inlet Historical Society and, among other things, helped organize a 1994 exhibition and international symposium celebrating the bicentennial of Captain George Vancouver's voyage to Alaska. He also helped organize a 2002 year-long celebration about Arctic and Antarctic exploration that focused on the 1907-09 Shackleton expedition, and more recent celebrations of Alaska statehood. He was coeditor and contributor to the Vancouver symposium papers, *Enlightenment and Exploration in the North Pacific 1741-1805*, University of Washington Press, 1997. More recently, he authored *Captain Cook in Alaska and the North Pacific*, Todd Communications, 2008. A fourth generation Californian, his principal leisure pursuit is the early history of the west coast of North America, from California to Alaska.

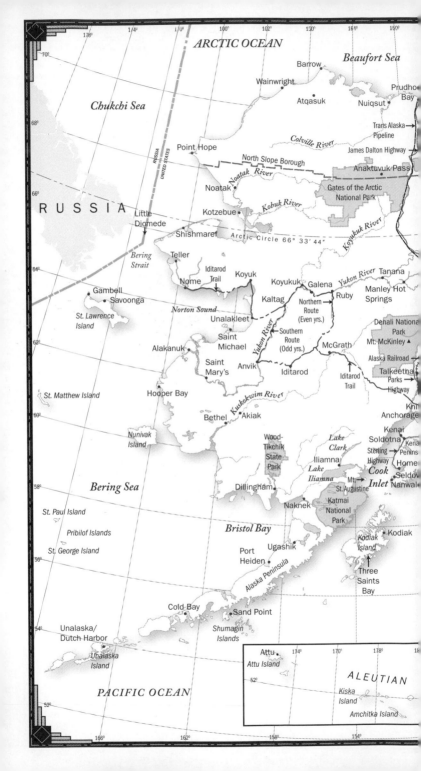

Alaskan History

ARCTIC OCEAN

Beaufort Sea

Kaktovik

Arctic National
Wildlife Refuge

Arctic Village

Fort
McPherson

Inuvik

CANADA
UNITED STATES

True north 23° *Magnetic north*
N

| 0 | 100 | 200 |
Miles
| 0 | 100 | 200 |
Kilometers

Yukon River Fort Yukon

Arctic Circle 66° 33' 44"

Circle

Yukon

C A N A D A

Fairbanks

Eagle

River

Nenana
Parks
Highway

Delta
Junction

Chicken

Dawson City

Cantwell

Paxson

ichardson Highway

Tok

Alaska Highway

YUKON

Ross River

Glenn Highway

Glennallen

Carmacks

Vasilla
Palmer

Chitina

Kennecott
McCarthy

Whitehorse

Alaska Highway

Valdez

Trans Alaska
Pipeline

Haines
Junction

Whittier

Prince

Cordova

Mt. St. Elias

White Pass &
Yukon Route Railway

BRITISH
COLUMBIA

Seward
Highway

William

Dyea

Skagway

eward

Sound

Yakutat

Haines

CANADA
UNITED STATES

Juneau

Lituya
Bay

Glacier Bay
National
Park

Gulf of Alaska

Petersburg

Sitka

Wrangell

PACIFIC OCEAN

Ketchikan

Prince
Rupert

I S L A N D S

Atka

Adak

Atka Island

Adak Island

Map by
RON ENGSTROM

Chapter One
Alaska's First People

*H*uman history in Alaska extends to as many as 20-40,000 years ago when it is believed the first humans crossed the Bering Land Bridge from what is now Siberia. Many of these first people continued south, but eventually the first humans came to stay. Today Alaska Natives comprise fifteen percent of the total population. They maintain traditional customs in hundreds of villages that characterize the original essence of Alaska, such as subsistence hunting, fishing and arts and crafts. Although Native culture and traditions define the 49th state, recent migrants have diversified local tradition and now offer a cosmopolitan and international appeal.

The Bering Land Bridge and the Settlement in America

Many scientific theories exist about settlement of the Americas. Ideas change as new investigations expand the understanding of human migration. Scientists assume that enough seawater was frozen in the Arctic and Antarctic ice caps during recent ice ages that the shallow sea floor of the Bering Sea became dry land. The Bering Land Bridge was broad grassland that joined present-day Alaska and eastern Siberia for centuries. So despite varying assumptions it is still believed that people who crossed the Bering Land Bridge first settled America from Asia.

However, the pattern of migration, its timing, and the place of origin is in debate. As new discoveries come to light, particularly when ancient sites are found and dated, past hypotheses are reconsidered and new theories constructed. Nonetheless, the evidence still suggests that a widespread habitation of the Americas occurred during the end of the last glacial period some 15-20,000 years ago. Some theories suggest this was simply the last or most significant wave of settlement and that the first group of people entered the hemisphere at a much earlier date, possibly 20-40,000 years ago.

The exact time that humans settled in Alaska is not known, but some suggest permanent settlements occurred about 10-12,000 years ago. As Alaska was settled, four distinct cultures developed: (1) the Aleut and Alutiiq in the Aleutian Islands and Southcentral Alaska, (2) the Tlingit and Haida in Southeast Alaska, (3) the Athabascan Indians in Interior Alaska, and (4) the circumpolar Eskimo, known today as the Yup'ik and Iñupiat of western and northern Alaska. Alaska history should first be considered by understanding the characteristics of these distinct cultures before their first contact with Europeans in the eighteenth century.

Aleut (Unangan) and Alutiiq

The Aleut are maritime people who developed specialized skills to survive in a harsh climate. Although their location allowed them easy access to fishing and hunting, they showed exceptional skill in harvesting salmon and halibut with spears, nets, hooks and lines. They used nets and harpoons to capture larger mammals, such as whales, seals, sea lions and sea otters. Their most ingenious invention was the skin kayak or *iqyax*, which was capable of long journeys in dangerous seas. The Russians called kayaks *baidarkas*, the precursor of fiberglass kayaks in widespread use today.

Since the oldest known Aleut archeological site is located in the eastern Aleutian Islands, anthropologists believe the Aleuts traveled west from the Alaska Peninsula to settle in the 1,300 mile long island chain. Linguists

A Man of Oonalashka, 1776-1780, watercolor by John Webber from Captain Cook's third voyage. Mitchell Library, State Library of New South Wales (Ref: DL PXX 2/f.28).

believe the Aleut language separated from the earlier Eskimo languages about 4,000 years ago as the westward migration along the archipelago progressed. The name "Aleut" was given by Russian fur traders, but they know themselves as *Unangan*, "the coastal people."

Aleut hunters wore distinctive bentwood visors with sea lion whiskers, which provided protection from rain and sun. Skins from seal, sea lion, sea otter, bear, birds, squirrels and marmots were turned into clothing. Women and children did not hunt. Instead they gathered shellfish along the beaches and berries and other plants in the hills. They were well known for basketry, woven with geometric patterns in up to 2,500 stitches per square inch. They also sewed seal gut into watertight raincoats. Aleut society was stratified and the most respected were often mummified and treated with great ceremony at death.

A closely related culture is the Alutiiq, also called Pacific Eskimo or Sugpiaq, who

A Woman in Prince William's Sound, 1776-1780, watercolor by John Webber from Captain Cook's third voyage. Mitchell Library, State Library of New South Wales (Ref: DL PXX 2/f.27).

lived on the lower Kenai Peninsula, Kodiak Island and within Prince William Sound. Like the Aleut they lived a traditional coastal lifestyle, but also occupied inland villages on rivers and lakes. They subsisted on salmon, halibut and whale, as well as berries. Land mammals such as caribou, moose and bear were also present in their diet. Each settlement had defined territories. They traded and intermarried with the Aleuts, the Central Yup'ik of Bristol Bay, Dena'ina Athabascans and even the Eyak and Tlingit to the east. Like other Alaskan Native people, they were generally peaceable and have rich oral histories that tell of powerful spirits of animals and natural forces.

The traditional house of both cultures was a semi-subterranean oblong pit dwelling with wooden or whalebone frames and rafters covered by grass and sod. The Alutiiq called the houses *ciqlluaq* and the Aleut called them *barabaras* or *ulax*. For thousands of years, the homes provided efficient protection from unpredictable weather conditions. They were entered with

The Inside of a House in Oonalashka, 1776-1780, watercolor by John Webber, from Captain Cook's third voyage. Mitchell Library, State Library of New South Wales (Ref: DL PXX 2/f.34).

a pole ladder through the ceiling and were hard to distinguish from the surrounding terrain. Winter was a time for singing, dancing and feasting after the food for the winter had been gathered and stored. These ceremonies were held in large communal houses where performers wore elaborate costumes and carved wooden masks. People had tattoos and also wore bone labrets, body paint and other decorations.

The people thrived as independent cultures until the Russian fur traders conquered the Aleutian Islands after 1741. European contacts were not always hostile. In 1778 Captain James Cook encountered both Aleut and Alutiiq populations and left a considerable record. His first encounter was in eastern Prince William Sound, but his reports were more extensive in Unalaska, writing

> *These people [have] ... black eyes, small beards, and straight long black hair, which the Men wear loose behind and cut before, but the women tie it up in a bunch behind. ... the Woman's frock is made of Seal skin and the Men's of birds skins and both reach below the knee. This is the whole dress of the Women but Over this frock the Men wear a nother made of Gut which resists water and has a hood to draw over the head; some of them wear boots and all of them a kind of oval snouted Cap made of wood, with a rim to admet the head... They make no use of paint but the Women punctulate their faces slitely and both men and Women bore the under lip to which they fix pieces of bone, but it is as uncommon at Onalaska to see a man with this ornament as a women without it.*

Cook was fascinated by the bountiful harvest of fish and plants, as well as the construction of their homes. While some iron and pots had been acquired from the Russians, the Aleuts preferred traditional implements. "They did not seem to wish fore more iron or want any other instruments," Cook explained, "except sewing nee-dles, their own being made of bone, with which they not only sew their Canoes and make their clothes, but make also very curious embroidery."

The English noted the Aleuts had no weapons, a state imposed upon them by the Russians. "...we can-not suppose the Russians found them in such a defence-less state, but rather for their own security have disarmed them." The kayak was especially fascinating with its tight construction and maneuverability in the water. "The sleeves of his frock is tyed tight round his wrists, drawn close round his neck, the hood drawn over his head where it is confined close by his Cap, so that no water can pen-etrate either his body or into the Canoe." Cook also remarked on the ingenious engineering of the double bladed paddle and the fishing and hunting implements tied to the side of the kayak, including the "dart" used to spear fish and otter alike.

By 1799, when the Russian American Company was formed, probably half of all Aleut and Alutiiq males were hunting for the Russians, enslaved to pay tribute in furs to protect their families. Loss of life by drowning while hunting, warfare with the Tlingit and exposure to Western diseases decimated the population. By the 1820s those who survived found that their lives improved as Russians spread the Orthodox faith, embraced local culture and provided hospitals and health care.

Athabascan Indians of the Interior and Cook Inlet

The Athabascan Indians were hunters and inland fishermen who evolved as eleven distinct language groups along the Yukon, Tanana, Susitna, Kuskokwim and Copper rivers. They were semi-nomadic and lived in small family groups or clans, subsisting on salmon, waterfowl, rabbits, caribou and bear. They hunted with snares, clubs, spears and bows and arrows. In the winter they used snowshoes made of birch and rawhide. Clothing was made of animal hides, decorated with porcupine quills colored with natural dyes. Men's beaded jackets, women's beaded dancing boots, shell necklaces and beaded tunics were important ceremonial objects. Traditional tools were made of stone, antlers, wood and bone. Such tools were used to build houses, boats, snowshoes, clothing and cooking utensils.

They spent winters in permanent camps with a number of hemispherical homes covered with moose or caribou hides. In the summers they moved to fish camps to harvest marine resources. The clan system governed the intensive fishing period overseen by a *qeshqa* or chief. They were well known for multi-faceted use of the birch tree, which provided house frames, canoes, snowshoes, utensils and containers. They also perfected a storage technique to preserve late-run salmon in "cold storage" pits.

Like other Alaska Natives, their greatest tradition was sharing. Leaders were the best hunters and organized festivals to prove their ability to provide for the larger group. Clan elders made decisions concerning marriage, leadership and trading customs, but most tribes were matriarchal, tracing their ancestors through their women, rather than through the men. They formed partnerships with other communities and cultures as an intricate system of trade, diplomacy and exchange blossomed.

The Dena'ina Athabascans occupied the Cook Inlet region and had a more structured clan system. Linguistic and archeological evidence suggests that their territory was expanding at the time of European contact, occupying more than 160 camps and settlements. They had lived in the region for 2,000 years and were established along the Kenai Peninsula and Kachemak Bay in southern Cook Inlet by 1000 A.D.

Two women and children in Southcentral Alaska, 1898 (Dena'ina village of Tyonek). UAA-hmc-0116-series3a-44-3, Edwin F. Glenn papers, Archives and Special Collections, Consortium Library, University of Alaska Anchorage.

Captain Cook was the first European to encounter Athabascans when he met several parties of Dena'ina in upper Cook Inlet. These Natives were presumably members of the Kenaitze tribe. The most significant contact came when Lieutenant King took formal possession of the region on June 1, 1778. The Natives offered some salmon and two dogs in exchange for some iron. Fearing mischief, the British seized one of the dogs and "took it down to the boat and shot it dead in their sight," Cook reported, "which seemed to surprise them very much." This was not "wanton cruelty," Cook later explained, as the dog was simply shot to demonstrate the superiority of British firearms "to prevent any evil intentions they might form."

The sailors then displayed the flag, turned the turf, buried a bottle with some coins and papers and drank some port wine to the health of the king. The Natives quietly observed the British ceremony. Midshipman Gilbert explained, "We ... took possession of the Country in the name of His Britannic Majesty. About a dozen of the Natives were present and behaved very friendly but had no idea what we were doing."

A decade later Russian fur hunters came into Cook Inlet. Competition between fur companies was so intense that hostilities broke out in 1797. In the Battle of Kenai over 100 Dena'ina and 25 Russians were killed. The competitors soon over hunted the sea otter population and abandoned the region. Athabascans then enjoyed 80 more years of sovereignty until Americans arrived to search for gold after the Alaska purchase.

Tlingit, Haida and Southeast Alaska Cultures

Southeast Alaska people include the Tlingit, Haida, Eyak, and Tsimshian cultures. The Tlingit were the most numerous, dominating the area from Yakutat to Ketchikan, trading with related Northwest Coast people as far south as Washington State. The Eyak were located in eastern Prince William Sound, the Haida in southern Prince of Wales Island, and the Tsimshian emigrated to Metlakatla Island near Ketchikan during the

Chilkat Indians in dancing costumes, Alaska, ca. 1890. Courtesy of the Library of Congress Prints and Photographs Division, LC-USZ62-101325.

territorial period from near Prince Rupert, British Columbia. They shared a bond with other Northwest Coast people from British Columbia to coastal Washington.

The social organization was defined by the status obtained through wealth, particularly the potlatch. A family or chief would improve his status by giving away food and possessions, usually in winter when there was more time to devote to music, dance and spiritual ceremonies. They told stories of clan history through art, music and storytelling, featuring depictions of fish, animals and mythical creatures. The potlatch was banned in Alaska during the late nineteenth century, largely at the urging of missionaries and government agents who did not understand its purposes. These people married outside of their own group and, like many other Alaskans, traced their lineage from their mother. Slaves were usually captives from war raids on other villages.

Totems of Old Kasaan, a Haida village on Prince of Wales Island, near Ketchikan, ca. 1890. Box 278, Donated Materials in the National Archives, Henry S. Wellcome Collection, 1856-1936. National Archives and Records Administration—Pacific Alaska Region (Anchorage), ARC Record 297711.

Despite frequent rain, the mild climate and plentiful resources of Southeast Alaska allowed them leisure time to devote to social pastimes, travel and trade. The world-renowned totem poles were carved to illustrate myths, honor the deceased and recognize tribal history. The people used animal fur, mountain goat wool, tanned skins and cedar bark for clothing. Hats were made of spruce roots and cedar bark. They built their homes from red cedar, spruce and hemlock timber and planks. The homes were quite large, accommodating 20-50 people, and each had a central fire pit and smoke hole. The villages would assemble in a single row of houses for easy access to fish-producing streams and give protection from storms and enemies.

Southeast Alaska produces many tall and massive trees, so wood was plentiful and the most important commodity. Houses, totem poles, daily utensils, storage and cooking boxes, canoes, ceremonial objects, labrets (worn by high status women) and clothes were all made of wood and wood products. The tools to make the wood into usable items were adzes, mauls, wedges, digging sticks and, after European contact, iron. Baskets were used for cooking and storage for clams, berries, seaweed and water. Woven mats were used as room dividers and floor mats, as well as to wrap the dead prior to burial or cremation. Salmon and halibut were harvested using weirs, fish traps, dip nets, hooks, harpoons and spears.

Besides the totem pole, the most distinctive cultural feature was Chilkat weaving, one of the most complex weaving techniques in the world. The name is derived from the Chilkat tribe in Klukwan. Traditionally chiefs wore Chilkat blankets during potlatch ceremonies. After European contact, robes were also made of blankets obtained from the Hudson Bay Company, adorned with glass beads and mother-of-pearl shells, along with buttons and abalone shells.

The first encounter between coastal Alaska people and Europeans came in 1741 with brief contacts during the Bering and Chirikov voyages. The Spaniard Bodega y Quadra had another brief contact in Bucareli Bay west of Prince of Wales Island in 1775. Although Cook was in contact with the Northwest Coast people in Nootka Sound on Vancouver Island, he did not encounter any Alaskans until entering Prince William Sound. So the first substantial European contact with people living in the Alaska Panhandle came when British, American and Russian traders sought sea otter furs in the late 18th century. Many of these contacts were hostile, particularly after Russians brought hordes of Aleuts to hunt sea otter in Tlingit territory.

Yup'ik of Southwest Alaska

The earliest known Eskimo cultures date to 7-8,000 years ago, having apparently evolved from people who migrated to Alaska from Siberia. About 2,000 years ago two language variations appeared. The Inuit language spread across northern Alaska, Canada and into Greenland, and the Yup'ik dialect developed in southwest Alaska. In Canada and Greenland, the term *Eskimo* is considered pejorative and has been replaced by the term *Inuit*. But *Inuit* is not used in Alaska, but instead *Iñupiat* refers to the people of the Northwest Arctic and North Slope.

The estimated Yup'ik population at the time of contact was 15,000. Most resided in the Yukon-Kuskokwim Delta and along the Kuskokwim River as separate Yup'ik and Cup'ik cultures. They lived on a mostly flat, marshy plain crisscrossed by large rivers, which they used as roads. Because this region is below the Arctic Circle, temperatures are more moderate and hunting and fishing continued most of the year. They still depend upon cultural traditions, including subsistence fishing, hunting and gathering for food.

The Yup'ik settlements and seasonal camps included extended families or groups of families, but they were small in comparison to other Native cultures. Roles and social rank were largely determined by gender and success as a hunter. The hunters, *nukalpiit*, usually became group leaders. Males lived in a *qasgiq*, where the men and boys lived, worked, ate, bathed and slept. Women prepared and brought food to the men. Ceremonies, singing, dancing and events usually occurred in the *qasgiq*, thus making it a community center. Women and girls lived in an *ena*, which was larger than the men's quarters to accommodate meal preparation. Both dwellings had a semi-subterranean winter entrance.

Women and children at Hooper Bay, showing sod home, located south of Scammon Bay in the Yukon-Kuskokwim Delta, ca. 1890. UAA-hmc-0731-87, Glenn H. Bowersox photographs and papers, Archives and Special Collections, Consortium Library, University of Alaska Anchorage.

Women were skilled in basketry and sewing. They stitched and fitted waterproof garments made of animal intestine and fish skins. The coats, called *parkas*, featured an attached hood and a ruff of wolf or bear fur. A customary and extraordinarily useful household tool was the *ulu,* a fan-shaped slate knife. The women also used the stone seal-oil lamp and sewing implements made from stone, bone and walrus ivory. Men's hunting tools included spears and harpoons, as well as bows and arrows. Most hunting implements were decorated with spiritual symbols. Snow goggles were an important technology, providing small slits to protect eyes from the glare of snow and ice. Skins of birds, fish and marine and land animals were used to make clothing. Hunting clothes were insulated and waterproof. The people used open boats called *umiaks* to hunt sea mammals. They were made of a driftwood frame and covered with tightly sewn sealskins. Sleds and dog teams were used for winter travel.

Captain Cook came in contact with the Yup'ik as his expedition sailed from Unalaska to the Arctic in July 1778. The inherent change from outside contact did not happen until much later, when Russian explorers and Orthodox missionaries arrived in the mid 19th century. This lack of contact helped maintain traditional Yup'ik language and subsistence harvests still in use today.

Iñupiat of the Northwest Arctic and North Slope

The Iñupiat are the "real people" from the Northwest Arctic and North Slope. They are sometimes grouped with the St. Lawrence Island Yup'ik because of a common language. The Iñupiat live in the most extreme climate in Alaska, if not the world. These hearty people worked to overcome the winds, ice, snow and temperature extremes to live a traditional lifestyle subsisting on whale, walrus, seal, polar bear, caribou and fish.

Inhabitants of Norton Sound and Their Habitations, 1776-1780, watercolor by John Webber from Captain Cook's third voyage. Mitchell Library, State Library of New South Wales (Ref: DL PXX 2/f.33).

They believed in reincarnation and the recycling of spirit forms from one life to the next, so names of those who recently died were often given to newborns.

The Iñupiat tended to live in small groups of related families with an estimated population at contact of about 10,000 persons. They lived in semi-subterranean structures that held 8-12 people with an underground tunnel entrance below the living level to trap cold air. During perennial winter darkness, life revolved around a seal-oil lamp made of soapstone or pottery, which provided light, heat and a fire for cooking. Homes were usually made from sod blocks, sometimes laid over driftwood or whalebone and walrus bone frames. They were generally dome-shaped. When the ground thawed most people constructed new structures as summer camps.

Traditional subsistence depended on the location and season, but most people hunted whales and other sea mammals, as well as salmon, herring, crab, halibut, cod and other whitefish. Traditional fishing gear included nets, traps made from branches and roots and hooks. Tools were made of stone, wood, bone and ivory for butchering, tanning and carving. The bow drill was used to start fires

and drill holes in wood, bone and ivory. Whaling captains maintained a sophisticated package of harpoons, lances, lines and seal bladder floats for hunting during the spring and fall migrations of bowhead whales. Seal-

St. Lawrence Island family, ca. 1890. UAA-hmc-0401-album1-16a, Philip and Retta Reed papers, Archives and Special Collections, Consortium Library, University of Alaska Anchorage.

skin floats and water-filled seal bladders were also used to attract whales and other sea mammals to shore and help float the carcasses after capture.

The people commonly used the *umiaq*, a large open skin boat, for travel and trade, as well as for hunting whale and walrus. Some *umiaqs* carried up to 15 people and a ton of cargo. The Iñupiat also used smaller kayaks for individual travel, as well as a basket sled and snowshoes for winter travel. Traditional clothing consisted of outer and inner pullover tops (*kuspuks*); and outer and inner pants, socks and boots. The woman's pullover had a hood for carrying small children. Tops and pants were made of caribou skin and gloves were made from various skins, with the fur turned inside and usually connected with a leather strip around the neck. Waterproof outer garments were made from sea-mammal intestines.

Given the remote location, whalers from New England had the first extended contact with the Iñupiat in the late 19th century. This lack of contact helped maintain many important traditions in the region to this day.

Chapter Two
European Discovery of Alaska

In April 1794 two ships under the British flag sailed into Cook Inlet in cold and treacherous conditions navigating past boulders, mud flats, shoals, ice and swift-flowing tides. The 36 year old George Vancouver, who had spent his life at sea on Captain James Cook's second and third voyages, was told to resurvey Cook's River to prove it was not connected to the Mackenzie River. In a few days he confirmed there was no passage to Canada, substituting the name "Cook's Inlet" for "Cook's River," the name given to honor the great captain by the British Admiralty. The voyage of Captain Vancouver not only resolved the speculations of the armchair geographers in Europe, but also completed the first exhaustive survey of Alaska, the last uncharted temperate region of the world.

First Europeans in Alaska

The Russian Empire had little interest in the North Pacific until Tsar Peter the Great came to power in the late 17th century. He created a modern navy and asked Vitus Bering, a Dane, to learn about Russia's proximity to America. The hardships of Siberian travel and the logistics of Bering's two overland trips 6,000 miles from the Russian capital overshadowed his accomplishments at sea. In his first expedition, after three and a half years en route, Bering sailed north from Kamchatka in July 1728, rounding the tip of Siberia. Although it was only a few miles away he rarely saw the Siberian coastline because of constant rain and fog. So he passed by the opposite coast of Alaska without knowing it was there.

He then proposed a second expedition. His first command used one hundred men; the second would require more than three thousand. In June 1741, the *St. Peter*, under the command of Captain Commander Vitus Bering, and the *St. Paul*, under the command of Captain Aleksei Chirikov, sailed for America. The ships soon separated in a storm, continuing toward America as separate voyages.

Chirikov's vessel reached the west side of Prince of Wales Island in six weeks. They found the shoreline steep and rocky, but could not find a safe harbor. Ten of the crew were sent for water in a large bay south of Sitka, but no landing signal was given and they did not return. After five days a fire was spotted, so a carpenter and caulker were sent to the same place in the remaining shore boat. Like the first party they were never seen again. Chirikov was certain local people had killed his men, but thousands of miles from home without shore boats he abandoned the sailors and returned to Siberia. Short of water and overcome with scurvy, the expedition was fortunate to find Kamchatka in early October.

As the *St. Paul* made its first landfall in southern Alaska, the *St. Peter* was several hundred miles to the north, sailing in cloudy, drizzly weather in the Gulf of Alaska. Just after noon on July 17, a high, snow-covered volcano appeared out of the haze. Since this was St. Elias day, Bering named it Mount St. Elias. They soon found Kayak Island where Bering sent his boats for water and to give the German naturalist Georg Steller time to investigate. In just ten hours Steller feverishly collected plants and examined abandoned Native homes. He presumed the Americans were related to the Natives of Kamchatka and speculated on their ancestral crossing. He wanted to stay longer, but Bering decided to sail with the onset of a fair wind, setting his return course in fog, rain and wind.

In two months they only retraced one-third of the route. Despite Steller's ministrations of shore weeds, the crew was overwhelmed by scurvy and sailors began to die every day. They approached an unknown island and were driven mercilessly onto a reef. Once ashore they slowly recovered, but Bering was too frail and weak. On December 8, 1741, after most of the survivors had regained their health, he died. A driftwood cross was erected and the forsaken place was named Bering

Island. The winter on Bering Island was not as desperate as the final days of the voyage as the survivors lived on sea otters. In the spring they built a small boat from the wrecked *St. Peter* and reached Siberia in two weeks. The sea otter pelts carried by the crew initiated a new compulsion among the Russian fur hunters to conquer these islands and their inhabitants.

Russian and Spanish Colonies on the Northwest Coast

As soon as Bering's crew returned, fur hunters or *promyshlenniki* (traders) left Kamchatka to conquer the Aleutian Islands in high risk expeditions to bring sea otter furs to the Orient. As each island's treasure of furs was wiped out the hunters sailed further east along the Aleutian chain. Each venture was like the Russian conquest of Siberia. After a brief fight, Aleut families were held hostage to force the male hunters to kill as many sea otters as possible. In the first twelve years two-dozen expeditions harvested millions of rubles in furs and the local sea otter populations were decimated.

The Voyages from Asia to America, depicting the Bering/Chirikov voyage tracks, projecting the Alaska coastline toward Kamchatka, and confirming the existence of a body of water between Asia and America. This Russian map was published in 1758 by Gerard Fridrikh Mueller, a German cartographer working in St. Petersburg, and was printed in English by Thomas Jeffreys in 1761—two decades after the Bering/Chirikov voyage. The British Library Board, 981.e.17.

The advancing Russian merchant fleet had the attention of Spain, particularly after the 1758 publication of the Mueller map of the Bering-Chirikov voyages. The Spanish considered the area their domain, so they appointed a new viceroy to push their rule to the north. He enlisted Junipero Serra, president of the Franciscan missions in Baja California, to establish missions in Alta California. They assumed settlements of Christianized Indians would repel Russian efforts to colonize the coast. Two ships headed up the coast from Mexico in 1769. Despite local resistance, Serra soon founded Mission San Diego de Alcala and then sailed to Monterey to establish a second mission. In the following years he was the dominant influence in the colony, founding nine missions and four presidios before his death in 1784.

Not satisfied with these meager colonies, the viceroy commissioned secret explorations to take possession of lands north of California. In 1774 Juan Perez reached the southern capes of Alaska before returning to California. Perez did not land because of hostile weather but he also did not find any Russians. The viceroy dispatched Bruno Heceta from Mexico in 1775. The 36 foot schooner *Sonora*, under the command of Juan Francisco de Bodega y Quadra, accompanied Heceta. Near the mouth of Washington's Quinault River, Natives ambushed six men off the *Sonora*. While Heceta took the sick and injured back to Monterey, Bodega set course to the northwest. Although short on water and rations, he reached the latitude of Lituya Bay before winds and high seas forced a retreat. The viceroy gladly learned there were no Russians and that Spanish claims to the north appeared intact.

Although the Russian occupation of the North Pacific was not as extensive as the Spanish expected, the advance of the *promyshlenniki* would soon yield permanent Russian colonies in Alaska. Grigor Shelikhov soon outfitted three ships that reached the southeast coast of Kodiak in 1783. This treeless corner of the island was "Three Saints Bay," the first Russian settlement in Alaska. The closest colony to the south was the tiny presidio and mission of San Francisco, founded just eight years before.

Voyages of the Enlightenment

In the last half of the eighteenth century many Europeans, especially from England and France, considered themselves the most civilized people in history. They believed it was their obligation to explore and illuminate the uncivilized world. This view guided the era of the Enlightenment, as the "light" of science would help informed and open minds improve mankind. Captain James Cook sailed at the height of this Age of Enlightenment. No one matched Cook's exploits in his three separate voyages charting the Pacific. He disproved the existence of the great southern continent, found the Hawaiian Islands and established that New Zealand was two large, narrowly separated islands. He also was the first to traverse the fertile eastern shore of Australia, setting in motion British settlements near modern day Sydney.

He sailed to the West Coast on his third voyage in 1778 to find the elusive Northwest Passage. Among the crew were Bligh, Vancouver, Dixon, and Portlock, who all gained notoriety as captains in their own right. Charles Clerke was the captain of the consort vessel and John Webber was the official artist. Cook's crew was a roster of the finest seamen and scientists of the British Nation, many of whom wrote of their exploits with the captain after Cook's untimely death in Hawaii in February 1779.

When Cook reached the Oregon coast, hail, sleet, fog and howling winds greeted his advance. He missed the Columbia River and Juan de Fuca Strait, and then put into Nootka Sound on Vancouver Island's west coast. As the sailors came to shore the cedar plank canoes of the local people surrounded the ships. Cook found

Webber's drawing of a sea otter in Nootka Sound (west coast of Vancouver Island), which helped stimulate the rush for fur along the Northwest coast and Alaska, nearly wiping out the population. Sea Otter, 1776-1780, watercolor by John Webber from Captain Cook's third voyage. National Library of Australia, http://nla.gov.au/nla.pic - an 2668094.

these people less attractive than the Polynesians. Most were covered with dirt and grease, but their music was pleasing, especially when paddling in cadence, and their carved wooden masks reflected extraordinary craftsmanship. Their principal interest was trade, and they bartered with the sailors for iron, offering animal skins, fishhooks, weapons and carved masks in exchange.

They again met bad weather until they reached Mount St. Elias. Cook was to follow the coast to the Arctic, but he found the coastline trending first to the west, then to the southwest. He had the latest Russian maps, suggesting islands and passageways separated Alaska from North America, but the continent bulged to the west. Soon he entered a large bay, which was later called Prince William's Sound. Here the ships met several dozen Natives who reminded Cook of Greenland Eskimos. They wore sealskin clothing and wore unsightly bone labrets on their lower lips. Their vessels were the sleek kayaks and larger skin-clad umiaks.

Leaving Snug Corner Cove, Cook coasted along the Kenai Peninsula, soon reaching a wide gap of open water fifty or sixty miles across. Cook and Bligh were certain it was not a passage to the Arctic, but the other officers were joyous, assuming this was

A View of Snug Corner Cove in Prince William's Sound, 1776-1780, watercolor by John Webber from Captain Cook's third voyage. Mitchell Library, State Library of New South Wales (Ref: DL PXX 2/f.25).

the beginning of a great inland sea. After several days sailing north in wind and tides they reached Fire Island the nearshore landscape suggested they were at an end. Bligh went in a shore boat to examine the northeast arm and returned to report a navigable river for only ten or twelve miles. King was then sent with two boats up the southeast arm, but wind prevented progress so Cook called it River Turnagain. After

Sea Horses (Walrus), 1776-1780, watercolor by John Webber, from Captain Cook's third voyage. Mitchell Library, State Library of New South Wales (Ref: DL PXX 2/f.32).

a brief possession ceremony, they turned to the south, losing two weeks charting an inland sea they did not name.

Passing Kodiak and the Alaska Peninsula in fog, they finally found a passage through the Aleutians that offered clear sailing to the Arctic. As they passed Siberia they entered the Arctic sea where Vitus Bering turned around in his first expedition. Cook soon reached an impassable ice pack that he wrote was "as compact as a wall." Discouraged, the expedition returned to Unalaska for three weeks to trade with the local people and a few Russians. Although the crew returned the following year to test the ice pack again, Cook had been killed in a dispute over a shore boat in Hawaii.

Aware of Cook's departure from Europe, the Spanish viceroy decided to intercept him as he reached America. A year too late, in 1779 Lt. Ignacio de Arteaga sailed from Mexico. In July he reached Prince William Sound, taking formal possession at Port Etches, the northernmost point ever claimed by Spain. Despite Cook's presence in these waters a year

Webber's drawing of a polar bear. White Bear, 1776-1780, watercolor by John Webber from Captain Cook's third voyage. National Library of Australia, http://nla.gov.au/nla.pic - an 2668084.

earlier, the Spanish returned believing Cook had not reached Alaska and that the Russians were still confined to the Aleutians.

The French were the next to follow in the ill-fated

The Cook expedition was nearly trapped by the Arctic ice southwest of modern-day Barrow. The *Resolution* beating through the ice, with the *Discovery* in the most eminent danger in the distance, 1776-1780, watercolor by John Webber from Captain Cook's third voyage. National Library of Australia, http://nla.gov.au/nla.pic - an7723688.

voyage of Jean Francois Galaup, Comte de La Perouse. La Perouse was an accomplished French seaman who had risen through the ranks defeating British warships. In 1785 he was asked to mirror Cook, promoting science and French trade in a world expedition. While his principal geographic discoveries were near Japan, he was the second European to visit Hawaii and he gained new knowledge of the Gulf of Alaska.

La Perouse reached Mount St. Elias in July 1786 and the ships entered Lituya Bay. The local inhabitants were excited by the visit with such intense trade the crew posted a continuous guard to avoid theft. They found the local people living in large wooden sheds with fires in the center over which fish were smoked. The women adorned themselves with stone labrets and both men and women had extensive skill in wood carving, building canoes and even working with iron and copper. The French stayed four weeks. As LaPerouse prepared to leave two long boats made soundings at the outlet. Despite warnings about the tidal rip the small vessels were engulfed and 21 men drowned. In profound anguish, the crew erected a monument, with the inscription: "Twenty one brave sailors perished at the entrance to this harbor; whosoever you may be, mingle your tears with ours."

Overcome by the disaster, La Perouse made no further explorations until he entered Monterey Bay six weeks later, the first foreign ship to visit the California colonies. The French were surprised how few Spaniards controlled so many Indians within the mission enclosures. They were also disturbed by the drudgery imposed on the Indians, wishing that the friars cared as much for their material welfare as for their salvation. They sailed west to Hawaii, then Kamchatka. After a brief stop at Botany Bay, Australia, they were never seen again. For more than forty years, their whereabouts was unknown until the wreckage was found in the Fiji Islands. Local legend tells that the frigates were destroyed in a storm. The sailors were killed by sharks or the local people when they reached shore. The few remaining crew constructed a small vessel from the wreckage but were lost at sea.

In response to the British and French expeditions,

Anonymous, but presumably José Cardero, Return of Stolen Trousers; the Mulgrave Chief Asks for Peace (El cacique de Mulgrave pidiendo la paz), 1791. Museo de América, Madrid—N°. Inv 02259.

Spain outfitted a Royal Expedition commanded by Alejandro Malaspina with a host of botanists, cartographers, astronomers and artists. They arrived at Yakutat Bay in June 1791 to look for the elusive Northwest Passage. He named the inlet "Bahia del Desengano" (Disenchantment Bay), as glaciers blocked progress. Hundreds of Tlingit Indians arrived in wooden canoes for trade, offering fishing implements, domestic articles, or apparel for old clothing, nails, buttons and other prizes. But as time passed, the Natives concentrated on iron goods, and those not offered were soon pilfered. The Spanish gathered Na-

José Cardero, Port of Mulgrave (Yakutat Bay) and Lodging of the Indians (Puerto de Mulgrave y alojamiento de los indios), 1791. Museo de América, Madrid—N°. Inv. 02249.

tive weapons, articles of dress, manufactured items and other artifacts for display in Madrid. They even attempted to learn the local language.

Malaspina returned to California, writing a generous, if not simplistic report of mission life. He then sailed for Mexico and the Philippines. Returning to Spain, Malaspina was embroiled in political intrigue. Tried and convicted of treason, he was imprisoned and the manuscripts of the expedition went unpublished. The scientific momentum in Spain during the Enlightenment thus came to an abrupt end.

The Crisis at Nootka; Vancouver's Voyage

In 1784 the official publication of Cook's last voyage sent merchants and traders from a host of nations to the West Coast for sea otter furs. Nathaniel Portlock and George Dixon, who had sailed in Cook's last voyage, left in companion trading vessels the same month that La Perouse left France. Later James Hanna, then James Strange left from China in separate trading expeditions. Finally, John Meares was discharged from Bombay. In all, seven English trading expeditions arrived on the West Coast in 1786.

Dixon and Portlock benefited from a winter in Hawaii. But Meares, unaware of the severity of Alaskan winters, unwisely spent it in Prince William Sound. His desperate condition the next spring made it clear that the traders needed a more temperate port away from the Russian settlements in Alaska. Slowly the merchants centered activities at Nootka Sound. Captain Hanna was the first to enter the harbor in 1785, and soon Americans, Spanish, even Portuguese and Swedes, stopped at Nootka. The local chieftain, Maquinna, became a virtual gatekeeper of the trade as his small tribe acquired the treasures of Europe in exchange for sea otter furs.

It was at this time that Esteban Jose Martinez was sent from Mexico to report on the sea otter trade. After an internal dispute, the consort vessel abandoned Martinez and continued to the west, sighting the Russian outpost at Three Saints Bay on Kodiak Island and landing at Unalaska. They mapped seven Russian outposts, and reported 460 inhabitants. Meanwhile Martinez sailed for Nootka. When he arrived, he found that

Meares had already erected at least one building, so he constructed a fort to assert Spanish rule. James Colnett, Meares' partner, bitterly complained to Martinez about the fort, refusing to recognize Spanish authority. Insulted, Martinez arrested Colnett and he and his ship were hauled back to Mexico.

The Crisis in Nootka became an international incident. The British were enraged by the affront and, sensing a weakening Spanish position in world affairs, they threatened war. Although the Spanish had been to Nootka first, their claims their expeditions were always kept secret. So a truce was reached. In the Nootka Sound Convention of 1790, each country abandoned its claim to Nootka and reparations were paid to Mears and Colnett.

While the British were already planning an expedition to follow Cook, the Nootka Sound Convention gave added impetus since supervision was required to restore Meares' possessions. George Vancouver was chosen because of his experience in Cook's third voyage. His two ships carried 145 men, 40 fewer than on Cook's final voyage. He was to assist at Nootka, then undertake a detailed survey from California to Cook's River in Alaska. The theoretical geographers were still at work, particularly at Cook's River, and the Admiralty wanted to put all the theories to rest. Vancouver was given the most capable surveyors, astronomers and map makers of the day. He was instructed to survey every inlet on the coast. This formidable task was planned to take two years but it ultimately required a third season.

The ships sailed April 1, 1791, around Africa's Cape of Good Hope to Australia, New Zealand, Tahiti and finally Hawaii in eleven months. During the first survey season, landfall was in April 1792 north of San Francisco Bay. They passed the mouth of the Columbia River in flood stage and continued until entering the Strait of Juan de Fuca. There they met Robert Gray, commander of the Boston trader *Columbia*. Gray was soon to become the first captain to enter the Columbia River, which he named after his ship. As Vancouver reached the end of the strait the coastline led to the inner reaches of the islands and channels that make up today's Puget Sound. Using shore boats they performed dozens of coastal surveys, giving over three hundred names to coastal features. In July they explored what is now downtown Vancouver, Canada and soon completed the first circumnavigation of the island that bears his name.

After fruitless negotiations with the Spanish at Nootka, Vancouver left for California. While he sailed ahead his consort entered the mouth of the Columbia River, struggling past dangerous breakers and a sand bar. Gray had accomplished the task in May, reaching 20 miles upriver. Now the *Chatham* anchored and its shore boats went 100 miles upriver to modern-day Vancouver, Washington. Meanwhile Vancouver entered San Francisco Bay, the first foreign ship to visit the mission and presidio there. He then sailed to Monterey, where he was shocked by the deplorable conditions of the missions. He then sailed to Hawaii, where he established cordial relations with King Kamehameha.

In April 1793 they returned for a second survey season along Vancouver Island and into Southeast Alaska. Vancouver was in charge of a survey party near Ketchikan when a group of Tlingit surrounded his party. He attempted to fend them off before ten Natives were shot, the only bloodshed in the expedition's three years. The expedition returned that fall to chart the California coastline, then wintered in Hawaii. In February 1794 he left for Alaska to begin the third and final survey season. In Yakutat Bay he was disturbed by a Russian hunting expedition of 900 Kodiak islanders. He knew this would anger the Tlingit residents and destroy the sea otter population. By late August the survey was finished at Port Conclusion on the inner coast of Baranof Island. They returned to England the following year.

At four years, six months, Vancouver's expedition was the longest in the annals of British exploration. Despite minor outbreaks of scurvy and a few skirmishes with Natives, the expedition suffered just six fatalities, one-third the normal mortality rate in England at the time. Vancouver devoted the last two years of his life to the preparation of his journal, but he died before its publication. A century later William Dall said Vancouver's explorations "have not been excelled by any other navigator" and he found in the 1880s that Vancouver's charts were still the most trusted authority on Alaskan waters.

Chapter Three
Russian America

The Russian colony in America started with the un-coordinated invasion of the Aleutian Islands by fur hunters and not the deliberate expansion of empire. The tsar only intervened after half a century to grant a trade monopoly to Baranov and the Russian American Company to consolidate fur operations and improve revenue collection. When Baranov retired, the Navy and Orthodox missionaries assumed the oversight. Life improved for the local people but diminishing profits ended the venture in 1867 with Alaska's sale to the U.S.

Russian Conquest of the Aleutian Islands

After Bering's crew returned to Kamchatka with a treasure of sea otter, the occupation of all the Aleutian Islands progressed rapidly. The *promyshlenniki* were descendants of Cossack hunters who dominated the Russian steppes and now conquered the American frontier. Emelian Bassov arrived on Bering Island in 1743 with a few dozen men in a small "shitik" or crude flat-bottomed boat. Spending a winter ashore, they turned the island into a virtual killing ground, returning the following spring with 1,200 sea otter and 4,000 fur seal pelts. Other voyages soon followed, each like the conquest of Siberia. Rather than hunting sea otter themselves, the Russians forced the local people to work for them. The tsar insisted the island inhabitants be well treated, but there was no government presence so the encounters often turned violent. The *promyshlenniki* sailed to Copper Island near Bering Island east

36

of the Kamchatka Peninsula and the Near Islands, western most of the Aleutian Islands. This gave them enough experience to sail further away from Siberia, reaching Unalaska in three decades.

When Captain Cook arrived in Unalaska in 1778 the people were friendly and willing to trade. He wrote they were "the most peaceable inoffensive people I ever met with . . . remarkably cheerful and friendly amongst each other and always behaved with great civility to our people." But the British were outraged by the Russian occupation. David Samwell, surgeon on the *Discovery*, wrote, "The Russians have been obliged to use harsh Methods to bring the Natives of Nawanalaska & the other Islands about into subjection & to make them honest. They told us that they never forgave a Theft but always punished it with instant death. … the inhabitants of this Island are in a state of Subjection to the Russians," he continued, "and it should seem from what we observed amongst them that they are made to pay Tribute to their Masters, all their Arms of every kind are taken from them."

When the Alaska fur rush began there were about 15,000 Aleuts living in the Aleutian Islands and the Alaska Peninsula, but probably 80 percent perished during the first and second generation of Russian occupation. By 1867 harsh treatment and the ravages of disease reduced the population to less than one-tenth of the pre-contact number.

Russian American Company

Grigor Shelikhov established the first Russian settlement on the southeast coast of Kodiak Island in 1783. Three Saints Bay was a small village with a few dwellings, including a school and an orthodox church. Although his primary interest was furs, Shelikhov decided the education and conversion of the Natives would lead to peaceful and permanent colonization. He mounted expeditions into the far corners of the island, and then to Prince William Sound and Cook Inlet, returning to Kamchatka with a bountiful cargo of sea otter pelts.

There were two Russian fur companies at the time and they arrived in Cook Inlet almost simultaneously. The Lebedev-Lashtokin Company set up its first trading post at Kasilof in 1787 and a second post in Kenai four years later. The Shelikhov-Golikov Company set up a post at English Bay (now Nanwalek on the Kenai Peninsula) in 1784 and a shipbuilding site at Resurrection Bay in 1791, the site of modern-day Seward. Because the two companies were competitors, each used threats and kidnapping in a ruthless campaign to control the lives and fur harvesting practices of 4-6,000 Dena'ina Indians. The intense competition reached a crisis when the local people revolted in 1797 at the Battle of Kenai. All 25 Russians who lived at the fort were slaughtered, as well as about 100 Dena'ina who were under the control of the Fort's manager.

When the battle was reported to Russian authorities the warring companies were forced to merge and the Shelikhov-Golikov Company, renamed the Russian American Company, was formed after Shelikhov's death in 1799. Shelikhov's wife and son-in-law, Nikolai Rezanov, assumed Company operations. As part of a twenty-year agreement the Russian government required that they establish new settlements in Alaska and seek furs as far south as Vancouver Island.

Alexander Baranov and the Occupation of New Archangel

In 1790 Shelikhov hired Alexander Baranov to manage his Alaskan fur enterprise and from 1790 to 1818 he was the Company's chief manager in Alaska. When Baranov arrived the company was loosely controlled and harvested furs on Kodiak, Afognak and parts of Cook Inlet. Within a few years he consolidated operations on the northeast end of Kodiak Island, which he called St. Paul Harbor, where timber was available, at the present-day city of Kodiak. He also expanded operations to Unalaska, Cook Inlet and Prince William Sound.

There was competition from British and American trade with the Tlingit in Southeast Alaska so Baranov pur-

The Russian Headquarters on the Island of Kodiak (Die Hapt-niederlassung der Russen auf der Insel, Kodiak), ca. 1792. Courtesy of the Library of Congress Prints and Photographs Division, LC-USZ62-69566.

chased land from the Tlingit for a small trading post near Sitka. While Baranov was away, Tlingit warriors overran the fort in 1802 and killed 80 Russians and Aleuts. Two years later Baranov returned with Russian warships to retake the post. Although foreign merchants provided them with firearms to resist, the Tlingit could not withstand relentless bombardment and fled into the surrounding forest. From the village's ashes Baranov built the settlement of New Archangel, the capital of Russian America, modern day Sitka. The *Battle of Sitka* was the last major armed conflict on Alaskan soil between Europeans and Alaska Natives.

British and American ships continued to call regularly in Southeast Alaska, as the population of the Russian colonies was too small to control trade. Baranov had 149 men under his command in Kodiak when he arrived. In 1794 the Imperial government sent another 123 men, including teachers, artisans and peasants. By the time Baranov moved the capital to Sitka there were about 400 Russians in both cities. So the company relied on Native hunters to harvest the fur, as many as 1,500 hunters at a time, using overwork and systematic violence as

Portrait of Alexander Andreevich Baranov, first Russian Chief Manager of Alaska, 1790-1818. Alaska State Library, Portrait Collection, P01-2603.

tools of exploitation. In the seven years after the occupation of Sitka as many as 800 Aleut men lost their lives in battle, drowning in kayak accidents or illness en route. While the government never gave Baranov the right to impose punishment, the Aleuts were beaten and often killed if they refused to join hunting or raiding parties. Corporal punishment was only abolished after Baranov was removed as manager.

The Russians never fully colonized Alaska, clinging to the coastline in their quest for furs. Three-fourths of Alaska was still unmapped when Alaska was sold in 1867. Yet when Baranov retired at age 71, the Russian empire reached Fort Ross, California. The fort was founded to supply the northern colonies and as an advance base for the sea otter trade. It operated from 1812 to 1841 and, though mostly unsuccessful, was the site of California's first windmills and shipbuilding. The Russians also briefly operated a trading station in Kauai from 1814 to 1817.

The Russian Navy

The Russian Navy was an occasional participant in the conquest of Alaska. After the Bering voyage, the tsar did little to learn about his colony until Joseph Billings joined the Russian Navy. Billings was a mere seaman on Cook's third voyage but signed on to lead an expedition to Alaska. Starting on the Baltic, the march across the Russian landmass surpassed the expedition's accomplishments at sea. But they reached Kodiak Island and Prince William Sound in 1790 and returned with the first accurate maps of the Aleutian Islands and Alaska's west coast. They also compiled a rough census of the Native people and were the first to report the extensive abuse of the Aleuts.

In the nineteenth century the Russian government launched another expedition. Its principal purpose was to establish relations with the Japanese Empire, but they also wanted to resupply the Alaskan colonies. It was commanded by Ivan Johann von Krusenstern and Rezanov, the new Japanese ambassador. The expedition avoided the difficulties of a transcontinental march by sailing from the

Baltic in August 1803. When they reached Hawaii the consort vessel *Neva*, commanded by Urey Lisiansky, sailed for Kodiak. Learning the Tlingit had overrun Sitka he sailed to support Baranov's efforts to retake the capital, bombing the Tlingit into submission. After a year collecting furs, the *Neva* sailed for Canton, China in late 1805.

New Archangel (Sitka) during the Russian occupation, 1805. RG 95, Box 2 of 25, Historical Photographs 1906-94, Records of United States Forest Service, Region 10, Juneau. National Archives and Records Administration—Pacific Alaska Region (Anchorage), HS 0305.

Rezanov and Krusenstern were turned away by the Japanese and sailed for Kamchatka. While Krusenstern returned to St. Petersburg, completing the first Russian circumnavigation of the globe, Rezanov left on a company ship to inspect Alaska. They reached Unalaska in July 1805 and, after a brief stay in Kodiak, arrived in Sitka in late August. Rezanov was aghast at the miserable conditions in the Russian colonies. In October he purchased an American ship and all its contents when it arrived in Sitka. Soon these supplies were exhausted and he sailed to San Francisco for more.

When Rezanov arrived, the Spanish colonies in Alta California were just as crude and impoverished as those of Russian America. The friars had constructed 18 missions and nearly 20,000 California Indians were enclosed within their compounds, but there was no trade because the California ports were sealed from foreign visits. Rezanov decided the best solution for both the missions and the Russian colonies was a joint Spanish-Russian enterprise on the coast. As if to seal his diplomatic plans, Rezanov was soon captivated by the Spanish governor's fifteen-year-old daughter, Doña Concepción Argüello. The courtship was intense and in six weeks they agreed to be married after approval from the papal authorities in Rome.

41

After returning to Sitka with needed supplies in September 1806, Rezanov set off for Kamchatka, St. Petersburg and Rome to secure the hand of Concepción Argüello and to initiate the Spanish-Russian colony. But he was soon taken ill and died of fever and exhaustion in Siberia. The Spanish girl waited several years for his return before entering the convent. She only learned of his death thirty-five years later. Their story of unrequited love became a popular ballad, novel and rock opera in twentieth century California. But Rezanov's death meant even more to the meager colonies. The grand plans for coastal empire were never proposed to the governments and the fortunes of both colonies gradually collapsed.

The Russian Navy did not return to Alaska for another decade. Otto von Kotzebue, who sailed with Krusenstern, was placed in command of a modest expedition of twenty-seven sailors, including the artist Louis Choris. Kotzebue set out from the Baltic in July 1815 and circled Cape Horn before reaching Kamchatka. Two years later he found and named Kotzebue Sound and Cape Krusenstern on Alaska's northwest coast before returning to Europe. His voyage was the first to introduce Europeans to Alaska Eskimo or Iñupiat culture. It is also remembered for the striking Choris paintings of the cultures of the west coast of North America and Hawaii.

Reports from the von Kotzebue voyage forced Baranov into retirement. While information from the clergy of his mistreatment of the Aleuts contributed to his demise, the Russian government was mostly troubled by dwindling payments from declining sea otter harvests. In 1819 Baranov died at sea before his return to Russia. His

Louis Choris, Aleut in quiaq (kayak) off the coast of St. Paul with fur seals on the beach and the Russian ship *Rurik* in the background, 1817. Alaska State Library, Louis Choris Photograph Collection, P139-48.

death ushered in a new phase in the development of Russian America. When the Company charter was renewed in 1821, it stipulated that the chief managers, or governors as they came to be called, had to be naval officers.

The Navy enlarged the bureaucracy and improved relations with the Native people, but it had little ability to find profitable enterprises. The new managers attempted to hunt whales, mine coal and find gold, all without success. Their only profit came from trading for land mammal furs with the Athabascans along the Yukon River. In order to prevent competition from foreigners, the tsar attempted to exclude British and American traders from Alaska by extending the colony's boundary to Vancouver Island. But the colony could not survive on its own and in 1824 agreed that 54°40' north latitude would be the southern boundary of Russian territory, the southern reach of Alaska today. Russia also gave the British and Americans the right to trade along the Alaska coast for ten years, effectively ending Russian fur hunting operations. By 1839 they leased their fur gathering rights to the Hudson's Bay Company because they were unable to carry on trade with the Tlingit.

Pope Innocent and the Russian Orthodox Church

From the time the first colony was founded at Three Saints Bay, Shelikhov imported missionaries to introduce the local people to the Russian Orthodox faith. Inspired by Father Serra and other pastoral theology, the missionaries embraced the people and their traditions were assimilated into the religion. Orthodox liturgies and texts were translated onto the local language and Aleut leadership was encouraged to join in parish life. Soon the company had more than they bargained for, as the missionaries befriended the local people and reported any company abuse to the Russian government.

Father Ivan Veniaminov, who later became St. Innocent of Alaska, was well known throughout Russian America for creating a dictionary for hundreds of languages and dialects based on the Russian (Cyrillic) alphabet. Born in Siberia, he volunteered for service in Russian America. After spending a year in Sitka he went to Unalaska in 1824, where he developed an alphabet for the Fox Island Aleut language. He then translated Russian liturgical texts into the Aleut language and later worked with other translations for related languages in the region.

Portrait of Innokentii, Metropolitan of Moscow (1797-1879), called the "Apostle of Alaska." Courtesy of the Library of Congress Prints and Photographs Division, LC-USZ62-13144, 3c32144.

In 1835 he went back to Sitka to design and build the Orthodox cathedral. He had a reputation throughout Alaska for effective spirituality and warm relations with the Native people. He instructed them in carpentry, bricklaying and other skills. When a smallpox epidemic threatened Sitka in the late 1830s he helped vaccinate many people. He returned to Russia in 1839 where he was appointed the first bishop of Alaska.

He continued to serve in America and Kamchatka until 1859 when he was appointed Metropolitan of Moscow, the highest office in the Orthodox Church. In 1977 the Orthodox Church named him a saint.

The most visible trace of the Russian colonial period today is the presence of nearly ninety Russian Orthodox parishes in areas of

Cathedral of St. Michael the Archangel, 19th century postcard of the cathedral of the Russian Orthodox Church in Sitka. Courtesy of the Library of Congress Prints and Photographs Division, LC-DIG-ppmsc-02051.

the former Russian colony. Many were established after the sale of Alaska to the United States, as the church retained a vital interest in the Native people. These parishes are still a leading light for Native people, including several Athabascan groups in the Interior, very large Yup'ik communities, and most of the Aleut and Kodiak populations. The success of Orthodox religion is unlike many of the religious orders that followed and underscores the ability of the early Russian missionaries to merge local cultures with Christian beliefs and rituals, and particularly Veniaminov's achievement in presenting the Christian religion in print.

Native Life in Russian America; the "Creoles"

Conditions improved for the Aleuts and Kodiak Islanders after the Russian Navy assumed control of the American colony. Many of these islanders had been removed from their homes and sent as far south as California to hunt sea otter, a risky and dangerous venture that was responsible for the continuing population decline during the 1840s. To help address their health and safety, Veniaminov and the Orthodox Church established schools and hospitals for the local people and gave them jobs outside of sea otter hunting.

Because so many Russian fur hunters had taken Aleut wives during the rough period of early colonization, there were many children of mixed parentage. These children were known as Creoles, which was not a pejorative term, but instead expressive of the high status such people enjoyed. They inherited the rights of their father's

Church of the Holy Ascension, Unalaska, 1947. UAA-hmc-0506-series 4-7-25, Harris M. Whiting papers, Archives and Special Collections, Consortium Library, University of Alaska Anchorage.

name, social status, and property and assumed the status of full-blooded Russians in leadership positions.

When the Company received its third and final charter renewal in 1841, the creole status was given the force of law. Creoles were formally identified as "landed gentry" with rights to education and prominent positions in the company and government. In 1863 there were 2,000 in service throughout Alaska. They often took roles supervising full-blooded Russians in remote trading posts and were soon viewed as the principal managers of the colony. However, after the sale of Alaska they were disenfranchised. Labeled "half breeds" by white Americans, they were refused American citizenship. Many emigrated to Russia but others stayed in Alaska and were absorbed by Native communities.

The British and Americans in Russian America

Boston merchant traders overwhelmed the Russian colony after the turn of the century. The best known was Captain Joseph O'Cain, who like many others traded with both Tlingit and Russians in Southeast Alaska. He was equally comfortable trading guns for furs with the Tlingit while resupplying the Russian colonies with food and supplies. In time he became Baranov's ally, helping to transport Aleut hunters to California. In 1807 he was drowned in the eastern Aleutians while transporting California sea otter to the Orient.

In 1826, Sir John Franklin developed an ambitious plan to send a fleet of ships north of Alaska and Canada through unexplored waters. One group would search from the east; the other from the west. Franklin came from the east, but ice forced him to turn back in the Arctic Ocean. He did reach and name Prudhoe Bay. Captain Frederick W. Beechey of the British Royal Navy sailed *H. M. S. Blossom* on the westward leg through the Bering Sea. He hoped to join Franklin somewhere on the Arctic coast but the ice pack stopped him near Icy Cape. His crew worked a boat through leads in the ice pack to Point Barrow.

Eleven years later, Hudson's Bay Company traders Peter W. Dease and Thomas Simpson descended the Mackenzie River in Canada in an effort to complete Franklin's route. They were also stopped by Arctic ice. Simpson did not give up. Walking whenever he could not make use of Eskimo boats and open leads, he reached Point Barrow on August 4, 1837.

Beechey reported sighting whales in Arctic waters, stimulating American whalers to return by mid-century. Whaling was an important business of the era, as whale oil provided lamp oil and baleen was made into corsets and collar stays. By 1852 more than 200 American whaling ships hunted bowhead whales in the Bering Sea. Ships set out from ports on the East Coast for two years and took no notice of the Russians when in Alaska waters. In the fall they rounded Cape Horn and hunted in the southern Pacific Ocean until early spring. The ships then sold the winter's catch of oil and baleen in Hawaii before sailing to Alaska for the summer. They hunted whales in the Bering Sea and the Arctic Ocean until fall storms and ice forced them south, returning to the East Coast the following year.

Most whaling crews traded with Eskimos, exchanging tobacco, liquor and other items for ivory and furs. The whalers hired local people to work aboard ship. Men worked as dockhands and hunters, and women made clothing. This employment not only altered the annual hunting cycle but also brought the Iñupiat Eskimo people into contact with Western culture for the first time, disrupting their traditional lives forever.

Whaling in Alaska's waters continued for over a decade. The Confederate ship *Shenandoah* fired the last shots of the American Civil War in the Bering Sea. The ship was a raider sent out by the Confederate government in 1864 to prey on Union whalers. After cruising in the Pacific for whalers near Hawaii, the *Shenandoah* entered the Bering Sea in June 1865, two months after the war ended. Believing the war was still in progress, the raider attacked and destroyed most of the American whaling ships in the Bering Sea. When it was stalled by ice it turned south, learning months later that the war was over. It cruised for 13 months and covered 58,000 miles, burning and sinking 21 whaling ships after the war was over. This destruction of the whaling fleet, combined with dramatic losses of ships to ice, forced the commercial whaling industry to cut back and soon abandon Arctic whaling.

Decline of Russia on the Coast

By the 1860s the Russian government wanted to rid itself of its Russian America colony. Over hunting had severely reduced the sea otter population and the British and American traders were competing successfully for the fur that remained. In Southeast Alaska the colony was dependent on the Tlingit for food supplies and still feared hostilities. The brother of the tsar, Admiral-General Konstantin, argued that the fur resources of the Amur River basin near China were easier to defend and cheaper to supply than Alaska. So after the Crimean War (1853-55) and the heavy debt incurred from it, the tsar decided to sell Russian America.

Chapter Four
Seward's Folly

Alaska was an uncertain prize when purchased for $7.2 million by the United States government after the Civil War. Sea otter was the only known resource and it had been hunted to virtual extinction during the Russian occupation. The harsh climate and sparse population suggested Alaska would be a demanding, cash-strapped colony for years to come. It is no wonder Secretary of State William Seward was ruthlessly criticized for signing a treaty that acquired this uncertain real estate in the Far North.

The Russian Predicament

In 1856 Russia was near bankruptcy and feared losing its Alaska possession, so Tsar Alexander II was ready to sell. When the British declined, the Russians proposed a sale to the United States. In 1859 the Americans were in no position to negotiate given the imminent secession of the Southern states. Following the Union victory the Russian minister, Eduard de Stoeckl, renewed negotiations with Secretary of State William H. Seward. Seward was enamored by the opportunity to further expand the Nation's boundary, so negotiations quickly concluded on March 30, 1867. Seward initially offered $5 million, an amount Stoeckl was authorized to accept, but Stoeckl raised the price and they finally agreed to $7,200,000.00 or about 2.3¢ per acre.

Signing of Treaty of Cessation, March 30, 1867. A print from the painting by Emanuel Leutze showing the Alaska Purchase. Shown left to right; Robert S. Chew; William. H. Seward (Secretary of State), William Hunter; Mr. Bodisco; Baron de (Eduard) Stoeckl (Russian Diplomat); Charles Sumner and Frederick W. Seward. Alaska State Library, Alaska Purchase Centennial Commission Photograph Collection, P20-181.

The Russians said Alaska contained about 2,500 Russians at the time, including the creoles, as well as just 8,000 indigenous people under their control, or a total of 10,000 people within the colony. They also estimated another 50,000 Alaska Natives lived in the territory outside Russian jurisdiction. They had settled at 23 small trading posts along coastal Alaska, where a handful of merchants collected furs. There were only three permanent settlements: New Archangel (Sitka), Kodiak and in the Pribilof Islands.

Ratification and Enactment

When Seward announced the treaty, the pubic response was favorable because Americans still embraced principles of "Manifest Destiny." Some newspapers ridiculed Seward and editorialized against the purchase, suggesting it was "Seward's Folly" and that Alaska was "Walrussia." Horace Greeley of the *New York Tribune*, who coined the phrase "Go West Young Man," disliked Seward. He complained openly, writing:

> *Already we were burdened with terri-*
> *tory we had no population to fill. The Indians*
> *within the present boundaries of the repub-*
> *lic strained our power to govern aboriginal*

*peoples. Could it be that we would now, with
open eyes, seek to add to our difficulties by increasing the number of such peoples under our
national care? ... The territory ... lay away at
an inconvenient and a dangerous distance. ...
[Alaska] contained nothing of value but fur
bearing animals, and these had been hunted
until they were nearly extinct. Except for the
Aleutian Islands and a narrow strip of land
extending along the southern coast the country
would be not worth taking as a gift.... It was a
frozen wilderness.*

President Andrew Johnson called a special session
of Congress in April 1867. Radical Republicans opposed
the treaty because of their enmity for the President, but
Charles Sumner, chairman of the Senate Foreign Relations Committee, rallied the Senate to approve the treaty.
There is some evidence the Russians bribed some senators
to gain approval. Even so, Johnson's impeachment pro-
ceedings delayed funding. The House finally granted the
funds in July 1868.

Treasury Draft No. 9759, the check that paid for the purchase of Alaska, August 1, 1868. RG 217: Records of the Accounting Officers of the Department of the Treasury, 1775 – 1978. National Archives and Records Administration, Archives I Reference Section, Textual Archives Services Division, Washington, DC, ARC Identifier 301667 / MLR Number A1 48A, A1 48B.

The Aleut name *Alaska* was given to the new colony. The name is taken from the Aleut word *aláxsxaq*, an
object to which the sea is directed, in this case the Alaska
Peninsula. This is sometimes loosely translated as "great
land," but at the time was misunderstood as an Aleut ap-
pellation for their homeland. The transfer ceremony took
place in Sitka on October 18, 1867. Russian and Ameri-

can soldiers paraded in front of the governor's house. The Russian imperial flag was lowered and the American flag rose amid salutes and cannon fire. The Russians then vacated Sitka's few buildings, boarded a ship and sailed home. Only a few traders and Orthodox priests remained.

Today Alaskans celebrate March 30 as Seward's Day, the day the treaty was signed, and October 18 as Alaska Day, the day Alaska was transferred from Russia. With the purchase of Alaska, the United States acquired an area more than twice as large as Texas. Today it seems a bargain, but at the time few Americans embraced Seward's purchase. It was not until the Klondike gold strike in nearby Yukon, Canada that Alaska was seen as more than a "folly."

An American Possession

Shortly after Congress ratified the treaty, thirty ships sailed from the west coast to Alaska to initiate trade or begin colonial administration. Most travelled to the Russian capital at Sitka, but others visited trading posts at Wrangell, Kodiak, Kenai, Unalaska, St. Michael and the Pribilof Islands. The new colony was called "Indian country", under control of the Army and a few modest garrisons were built, supported by a few customs collectors and the occasional Navy ship to collect taxes. In 1880, the first census found 33,426 people, just 430 non-Native and 1,756 creoles, far lower than the 1867 Russian estimates.

Custom house, castle, and barracks in Sitka, ca. 1883 (showing Barnov's castle). UAA-hmc-0108-series8d-1, Fred Wildon Fickett papers, Archives and Special Collections, Consortium Library, University of Alaska Anchorage.

The discovery of gold in Canada's Klondike invigorated the moribund colony. Between 1890 and 1900, the population doubled to 63,500 as thousands joined the Klondike gold rush. Most of the "stampeders" considered the move temporary but stayed. Even though most of the gold was played out by 1910 the population remained at gold rush levels. But it would take a world war several decades later for Alaska's population to exceed 100,000 for the first time.

During the late nineteenth century most Alaskans lived near the ocean or along major rivers where ships could provide supplies and transportation. Later, as newer transportation methods emerged, communities grew up next to railroads, roads and eventually airfields. Most of the new settlements were established during the gold frenzy at the turn of the century. Juneau began as a mining camp in 1880 and Douglas, across the channel, was founded a year later. Hope and Sunrise on the Kenai Peninsula, Circle City on the Yukon River, and Council on the Seward Peninsula started as mining camps before 1898. Supply camps like Dyea, Skagway and Valdez were built along the routes to the Klondike. Gold camps, such as Nome and Fairbanks, survived while others such as Iditarod and Chisana did not.

In addition to new mining towns, communities like Ketchikan began as fishing villages and Homer started as a cannery site and coal depot. There were several mission stations, such as Haines and Bethel. In Northwest Alaska, whaling stations were established at Barrow and Wainwright. The Army built Alaska's first telegraph system at the turn of the century, a 1,900 mile long route connecting six army posts across Alaska to the Bering Sea. An adjoining road went from Valdez to Fort Egbert, the army's headquarters near Eagle on the Yukon River. Small communities grew around telegraph stations along the route. Roadhouses were built to serve workers and travelers, including mail carriers. Seward was founded as the southern end for a road that would cross the Kenai Peninsula and then head north to Fairbanks. Cordova was the seaport for the Copper River and Northwestern Railroad that brought the rich Kennicott copper out of the Wrangell Mountains.

Commercial fishing gained a foothold in Bristol Bay and the Aleutian Islands. Packing houses salted cod and herring and salmon canneries were opened. Whaling and the harvest of fur seals and sea otters also continued after the American purchase. Many non-Native settlers expanded harvests of other species into the Interior and Arctic Alaska, further exploiting the fur bearers, fish and other game on which Natives depended.

Exploration of Alaska's Interior

Vast regions of land were still unexplored in 1867 and the federal government sought better maps and an understanding of the resources, geology and environment of the new territory. In 1865, Western Union started a telegraph line across Alaska to the Bering Strait. Robert Kennicott led the survey for the project. After he died, William H. Dall took charge, conducting the first survey and scientific study of the Yukon River. While the overland telegraph project was later abandoned, Dall returned to Alaska many times, recording and naming geological features. "Dall's porpoise" and "Dall sheep" were two species named in his honor.

The Alaska Commercial Company and the military also contributed to the growing exploration of Alaska,

Members of the Copper and Tanana Rivers Expedition, 1885. UAA-hmc-0108-series8b-1, Fred Wildon Fickett papers, Archives and Special Collections, Consortium Library, University of Alaska Anchorage.

as small parties of trappers built trading posts and there were periodic Army investigations. In a four-month journey in 1883, Lt. Frederick Schwatka and his party of soldiers crossed Chilkoot Pass, built a raft and traveled on connecting lakes and rivers down the Yukon River to Saint Michael on the Bering Sea. Schwatka collected information on the people and resources and wrote popular books about his trip. A year later the Navy explored from the

Kobuk to the Colville Rivers in Northwest and Arctic Alaska and made the first map of the region.

Schwatka's route began in Canada, so the Army looked for a corridor that originated in Alaska. In an expedition that rivaled Lewis and Clark, Lt. Henry T. Allen and four others undertook an overland trek in 1885 from the Gulf of Alaska near Cordova to the Bering Sea. They found the terrain so overwhelming they abandoned their horses and provisions, deciding to live off the land instead. In the first month they ascended the Copper River drainage to its source in interior Alaska. They might have starved if Ahtna chief Nicolai had not given them food.

Continuing north, they crossed the Alaska Range to the Tanana River valley, following that river to where it joins the Yukon River. Allen and one of his men then portaged to the headwaters of the Koyukuk River, descending to the Yukon again, finally crossing the Yukon Flats to Unalakleet on the Bering Sea coast, emerging at the trading post at Saint Michael. In five months Allen explored 1,500 miles of wilderness and charted the courses of the Copper, Tanana, Koyukuk and Yukon rivers. This unparalleled achievement greatly advanced the nation's understanding of Alaska's geography.

In 1898, the federal government announced a systematic topographic and geologic survey of Alaska. Alfred Hulse Brooks was appointed to find "the first clue to the geography and geology of the part of Alaska north of the Yukon Basin." Between 1899 and 1911 he lead or actively supported six major reconnaissance expeditions that traversed the Brooks Range and mapped its topography and geology. He also published annual reports of Alaska's mineral resources for the United States Geological Survey (USGS) nearly every year from 1904 to 1923.

Nineteenth Century Transportation

In the nineteenth century Alaska was only connected to the rest of the world by ocean travel. The challenges of remoteness, few people, seasonal markets, small ports, inadequate facilities and navigational problems

S. S. *Princess May* wrecked on August 5, 1910. Courtesy of the Library of Congress Prints and Photographs Division, LC-DIG-ppmsc-01752.

limited the number of shipping companies. Only the Canadian Pacific and the Alaska Commercial Company provided the service, usually sailing during summer months to Southeast Alaska ports and selected trading posts. Such travel was perilous due to uncharted hazards and unpredictable weather. Prior to 1900 the government made little effort to chart key channels and landmarks even though there were more than 300 accidents in the Inside Passage during 1898-1900 alone. Finally two lighthouses were constructed and the Navy started to mark underwater hazards. Even with these aids, losses averaged about 24 ships each year until World War II.

In 1910 the *Princess May* ran aground on Sentinel Island in Lynn Canal. She was steaming at full speed in the early morning in heavy fog southbound from Skagway when she slammed into the unseen island. Fortunately the lifeboats were lowered and the 80 passengers and 68 member crew were safely evacuated to a nearby island. But the tide went out and

C.P.R. Co. *Princess Sophia*, which sunk with all aboard. UAA-hmc-0428-series6-f3-9, Howard and Mabel Jonish papers, Archives and Special Collections, Consortium Library, University of Alaska Anchorage.

the ship was left high and dry before it was refloated. After shore side repairs it remained in service for another nine years.

Another Canadian Pacific steamship, the *Princess Sophia*, was not so lucky. On October 25, 1918, it sank with the loss of all 343 passengers after grounding on Vanderbilt Reef in Lynn Canal. The company refused assistance from nearby Juneau residents to evacuate the vessel and, with little warning, a storm developed and the wind and waves spun the vessel into deep water. It sank like a rock. All the passengers and crew drowned; only a dog survived. For several months bodies washed up as many as thirty miles from the wreck. It was

The stern-wheeler *Yukon* headed up the Yukon River at Eagle, Alaska in 1917. Curtis R. Smith Photographs, UAF-1997-59-22, Archives, University of Alaska Fairbanks.

the worst maritime accident in the history of both British Columbia and Alaska.

The Alaska Commercial Company also operated stern-wheelers in the Yukon River beginning in 1869. Each paddle steamer would push two loaded barges upriver to Fort Yukon once or twice a year. Operating between May and September, the lumbering vessels carried supplies to trading posts, took furs to markets and moved freight, fur traders and prospectors up and down the river. Once word spread that gold had been discovered in the Klondike at the turn of the century many more steamboat companies arrived. Gold fever meant a boat could pay for itself on a single trip upriver, commonly hauling hundreds of passengers and tons of freight from St. Michael to Dawson in two weeks.

Meanwhile fishing became a significant seasonal commercial enterprise for Alaskans. In 1878 businessmen built the first two canneries at Klawock and Sitka. In 1883 the Arctic Pack Company established a cannery at Nushagak Bay in Bristol Bay, where they were able to exploit the immense runs of sockeye (red) salmon. Two years later the Alaska Packing Company opened a cannery across the bay, and by 1908 ten canneries ringed Bristol Bay. Soon the first canneries were established on Kodiak Island. Private fleets of ships operated by these large salmon canners were the only alternative to reach Alaska. These ships transported workers and supplies from West Coast ports to canneries at the beginning of the fishing season and took the workers and canned salmon back at the end of the season. The Alaska Packers Association, known for its "Star Fleet" of square rigger sailing ships, was best known in this early era of Alaska salmon fishing.

In 1923 the Alaska Railroad began to compete in the transportation business after the rail line construction was completed. By the 1920s airplanes also carried freight and passengers throughout Alaska. The combination of barges, which supplanted the stern-wheelers, the railroad, local bush pilots and a few airlines continue to serve as Alaska's principal means of transportation to this day.

The Pribilof Islands

The Pribilof Islands are a group of remote volcanic islands 200 miles from the Alaska mainland. The Russian Gavril Pribilof found them by accident in 1786, reporting sizable fur seal rookeries to a fur-crazed government. Uninhabited at the time, in the 1790s the Russians forced

Separating and Killing Seals in Pribilof Islands, 1888. Alaska State Library, Mrs. Allen (Agnes Swineford) Shattuck Photograph Collection, P27-070.

hundreds of Aleuts to the islands to harvest fur seals. For the three decades after the American purchase of Alaska, the islands were leased to the Alaska Commercial Company, which turned the rookeries into virtual killing fields of up to 100,000 animals each summer.

Although advised of the rigors of life in St. Paul, Libby Beaman followed her husband to St. Paul Island after he was appointed to supervise the fur seal harvest for the federal government. She was probably the first western woman to venture into these remote parts, staying the single winter of 1879-80. She described conditions in a journal published by her granddaughter after her death. She wrote of the horrors of the fur seal harvest and made drawings of the islands and wildlife, but by the middle of the harsh winter agreed she underestimated the hardships of Arctic life. Her diaries have been turned into a popular play featuring the hardships of the first non-Native woman in the Arctic.

In 1911 the North Pacific Fur Seal Convention was signed by Canada, Japan, Russia and the United States to bring the slaughter to a halt. Further Congressional restrictions in 1989 now limit hunting to subsistence uses by local residents. The people of the islands turned to other resources and today the population of about 700 depends on the annual snow crab fishery and halibut harvests. The islands also provide support services to commercial fishing fleets, a weather station and Coast Guard base, and considerable annual summer tourism from birdwatchers that come to view an estimated two million nesting seabirds.

The Harriman Alaska Expedition

In 1889 the wealthy railroad magnate Edward Harriman arranged for a maritime expedition to Alaska that included an elite community of American scientists, artists, photographers and naturalists. The Harriman Alaska Expedition spent two months steaming from Seattle to Siberia and back and published a series of volumes on their discoveries. Historians question why Harriman wanted to go to Alaska. Some think he wanted to develop Alaskan resources or build a railroad, though he said it was just a vacation. Others suggested he wanted to buy Alaska from the U.S. government or build a bridge that crossed from the Seward Peninsula near Nome to Siberia. Whatever his motives, Harriman outfitted a remarkable expedition to catalog Alaska, its people and resources.

The Two Johnnies. John Muir (right—holding wildflowers) and John Burroughs (left) studying Alaska glaciers during the Harriman Alaska Expedition. Photo taken by Edward S. Curtis. Alaska State Library, Harriman Alaska Series, 1899 Photograph Collection, P305-186.

Harriman refit a steamship called the *George W. Elder* with lecture rooms, an Alaska library, a stable for animals, taxidermy studios, and luxury staterooms. The passengers included John Muir, Edward Curtis, John Burroughs, George Grinnell, William Dall, and William Brewer. In addition, Harriman brought his extended family, maids, butlers and other servants, a medical team, a chaplain, hunters and packers, guides and taxidermists. Together with the crew there were 126 on board.

Newspapers ran front-page stories about the trip as the *Elder* launched from Seattle to cheering crowds. Their first stop was the Victoria Museum, then farther north to Vancouver Island, and then at Metlakatla, Skagway and Sitka. They saw the positive and negative results of the Klondike Gold Rush and cataloged plants, animals and marine creatures, as well as geological and glacial formations. They even recorded a native Tlingit song.

In a month they reached Prince William Sound, discovering an undocumented fiord in the northwest corner of the Sound they called "Harriman Fjord." They also

Harriman Alaska Expedition members pose on beach at deserted Cape Fox village, Alaska, 1899, with Tlingit totem poles in background. Courtesy of the Library of Congress Prints and Photographs Division, LC-USZC4-8288, 3g08288r.

found nearby "College Fjord," a vast inland waterway that includes five tidewater glaciers, five large valley glaciers, and dozens of smaller glaciers. The expedition included both a Harvard and Amherst professor so they named the glaciers after renowned east coast colleges (women's colleges on the western side and men's colleges on the eastern side) but they deliberately ignored Princeton. After sailing for Kodiak and Siberia, the expedition turned back for Seattle.

The expedition discovered 600 species that were new to science, including 38 fossils. They charted the geographic distribution of other species, discovered an unmapped fjord and launched the career of Edward Curtis, who was so concerned about the dying Native cultures he decided to photograph Native Americans in iconic photos revered to this day. At first John Muir found Harriman and his family overbearing. But the two became friends, particularly after Harriman helped Muir lobby Congress for National Park legislation. In gratitude Muir gave the eulogy at Harriman's funeral in 1909.

The most lasting legacy of the expedition was the formation of an interdisciplinary scientific team to assemble information about Alaska, its people and landscapes, enabling the assembled experts to work together for a common purpose. Such a complete record had not been made on any voyage to Alaska since the third voyage of Captain Cook. Their principal concern was the impact of the Klondike Gold Rush. They were outraged that gold seekers plundered both the landscape and the dignity of Native cultures.

Tourism Opportunities Today

There are at least four ways to experience the themes of the first years of the Alaska territory in different regions of the state. In St. Paul and St. George, visitors can observe northern fur seal rookeries and abundant nesting birds in one of the most unique and remote landscapes in Alaska, called the "Galapagos of the North." In Fairbanks visitors can appreciate the era of the paddle wheel riverboats that plied interior rivers before the end of the nineteenth century. The riverboat *Discovery* gives a tour of the Chena as far as the Tanana River and introduces visitors to Native anthropology and culture, Alaska geology and glaciology and riverboat history.

In Sitka the Sheldon Jackson Museum is a Native American museum located on the former campus of Sheldon Jackson College. It was the first museum in the territory when founded in 1887 and is currently owned by the State of Alaska. Jackson was a Presbyterian missionary who was committed to the Christian spiritual, educational and economic wellbeing of Native Alaskans, founding numerous schools and training centers. The museum celebrates his accomplishments with thousands of Tlingit, Iñupiat, and Aleut artifacts.

Finally, in Whittier, an hour's drive east of Anchorage, visitors can not only experience the new auto-friendly tunnel access to Passage Canal on Prince William Sound, but on a day cruise recall the discoveries of the Harriman Alaska Expedition in College Fjord over a century ago. Prince William Sound is one of Alaska's leading wilderness charms, a mixture of ocean, land and glaciers within a maze of islands, channels and bays.

Chapter Five
Gold Fever

*O*nce ballyhooed as forbidden and foreboding territory, the discovery of gold in Southeast Alaska, the Yukon, Nome and Fairbanks brought fortune seekers to the four corners of the vast frontier and forever changed Alaska.

First Gold Discoveries in Alaska

In 1848, the same year gold was discovered in California, Russians reported finding gold in streams on the Kenai Peninsula, but they did little about it. As the fervor for California gold panned out these rumors spread through eastern Sierra mining camps and stirred miners to seek their fortunes in the Far North. Working their way from California, prospectors first found gold in 1861 on Telegraph Creek in Southeast Alaska. After the Alaska purchase prospectors surged north. Within ten years another discovery was made in a Stikine River tributary in the Cassiar gold district. Other gold discoveries near Sitka led to the organization of Alaska's first mining district in 1879, as miners wanted their claims legally recognized because there was no civil government in the new territory.

The largest strike came in 1880 when a Tlingit chief led prospectors Richard Harris and Joe Juneau to the mainland east of Sitka. They found "large pieces of quartz, of black sulfite and galena all spangled over with gold" in a creek that is now called Gold Creek. On their first trip they mined a thousand pounds of ore. Hearing the news, Alaska's first gold rush overwhelmed the mining camp of Juneau, named after its discoverer. Two years later one of these prospectors,

John Treadwell, filed claims for hard rock gold deposits on Douglas Island, founding the Alaska Treadwell Gold Mining Company. Before these mines were abandoned fifty years later his company employed as many as 2,000 people and removed $67 million worth of gold. In twenty years the boom was so remarkable that Congress transferred the capital of the territory to Juneau.

Ten miners stand in a mine tunnel with shovels and mining tools at the 1500 ft. level, Treadwell Mine in early 1900s. Alaska State Library, Case & Draper Photograph Collection, P39-0872.

When claims in Southeast Alaska no longer yielded profits, prospectors chased the Russian reports about the Kenai Peninsula and found gold in Resurrection Creek. One miner reported panning 385 ounces in less than two months. The community of tents and cabins that sprang up at the mouth of the creek decided to name themselves after the youngest person to step off the next boat. His name was Percy Hope. Miners discovered gold nearby in Six Mile Creek and a new tent community was christened Sunrise City. Hope and Sunrise and the surrounding area soon swelled to 3,000 people.

But the boom faded as quickly as it started. In a few months speculators moved north along the creeks feeding Turnagain Arm. Originally called "Glacier City," Girdwood was founded as a supply camp for these placer miners. It was renamed for Colonel James Girdwood, a Scottish-Irish linen merchant who staked the first four gold claims in the Girdwood Valley along Crow Creek in 1896. Girdwood has expanded since those early days and today is a community of 1,500 residents. It is home to Alaska's finest ski resort and some of its best-known Olympians. Founded twenty years before Anchorage, it remained a separate city until 1975 when it was merged into the Anchorage Municipality.

The Klondike Gold Rush

As the gold discoveries in California and British Columbia played out, prospectors searched for gold and other valuable minerals in the countless drainages of the upper Yukon River. By 1896, when the Klondike discovery was made, an estimated 1,600 people were probing the upper Yukon, half of them grubstaked by fur traders. In August 1896 "Skookum Jim" Mason, a Tagish man of the Dak l'a Weidi Clan, a Canadian First Nations tribe, headed down the Yukon River to rendezvous with his sister and her husband, George Carmack, an American prospector. Jim's cousin, Dawson "Tagish Charlie," joined the group to go fishing. On August 16 the foursome found nuggets and rich placer gold deposits in the shallow riffles of Rabbit Creek (now Bonanza Creek), eight miles south of Dawson City in an area now managed by Parks Canada. At the time Dawson City was an Indian fish camp, but in a year it was overtaken by prospectors, suppliers, saloon keepers and prostitutes. It developed rapidly and untidily and for a short time became the biggest city north of San Francisco.

The two Tagish Indians later said one of them found the nugget while washing a dishpan. Regardless, further investigation revealed gold deposits "lying thick between the flaky slabs of rock like cheese in a sandwich." When his wealth was secure, Carmack left the Yukon and abandoned his Native wife and child. He married a "cigar store operator" from Dawson

Front Street, Dawson City, Yukon in 1898. Crowded street scene; two burros front and center carry signs advertising "Hegg's new gallery, will be open Aug. 24." Alaska State Library, Wickersham State Historic Sites Photograph Collection, P277-001-089.

and they retired comfortably in Seattle. Skookum Jim and Tagish Charlie returned to their homes in Carcross. Jim changed his name to James Mason, built a large house and continued prospecting. He died in 1916, leaving his considerable estate in trust for the betterment of his people. Soon the "Skookum Jim Friendship Centre" was founded in Whitehorse and it still operates as the oldest native organization in the Yukon. Charlie took another path. He built a hotel with his riches but drowned in 1908 when he accidentally fell off a nearby railroad bridge.

Word of the gold discovery in Bonanza Creek did not reach the outside world for a year when the first successful prospectors arrived in San Francisco and Seattle. The country was suffering a series of financial recessions and bank failures, so Americans already down on their luck rushed to the gold fields. About 80,000 people came north, mostly American novices, "cheechakos" in the local language, taking one of four routes to the goldfields: the Chilkoot Trail, the White Pass Trail, the all-water Yukon River route, or the Valdez Glacier Trail. About one-third turned back, but those who

arrived soon discovered they were too late to stake claims and also too late to leave again, stuck penniless in the frigid Yukon until the spring thaw of 1899.

Scales & Summit, Chilkoot Pass, Alaska in 1898. Prospectors, tents and piles of supplies cover the ground at base of mountain pass; other prospectors are shown ascending path to summit. Alaska State Library, Wickersham State Historic Sites Photograph Collection, P277-001-030.

Most of the adventurers took steamers from Seattle for the Alaskan towns of Skagway and Dyea at the northern end of Lynn Canal. They had the choice of two passes to the Yukon, the Chilkoot Trail, an old Native route that began in Dyea, or the White Pass route that began in Skagway and climbed to Bennett Lake at the headwaters of the Yukon River. The Chilkoot Trail was a shorter trip but had a considerably steeper climb. Photographs of the trail circulated throughout America to show the formidable struggle to reach the gold fields. The White Pass was preferred. It took a little longer but was at a lower elevation.

Skagway and the White Pass trail also had a severe crime problem, organized by the infamous Jefferson "Soapy" Smith, who became the region's underworld boss. Victims of the gang's confidence swindles had little recourse because Smith bribed the local marshal. A vigilance committee was finally formed and on the evening

Soapy Smith's Saloon, Skagway, Alaska in 1898. Jefferson R. Smith and Rev. Charles Bowers at the bar, four unidentified men in the background. Alaska State Library, Wickersham State Historic Sites Photograph Collection, P277-001-009.

of July 8, 1898 Smith was killed in a shoot out on the local dock. Smith's killer, Frank Reid, also died in the exchange of gunfire. While Smith's gang was rounded up and chased out of Alaska, the entire community attended Reid's funeral. His gravestone was inscribed with the words "He gave his life for the honor of Skagway."

Whichever route to the gold fields was selected, Canada's North West Mounted Police forced the miners to climb the selected route several times to ferry a ton of supplies, which the Canadians thought was necessary to endure the hostile environment for a year. These Mounties also forbade handguns from entering British territory. After reaching the pass, 25 to 35 miles from Lynn Canal, prospectors built rafts to take them the final 500 miles down the treacherous Yukon River to Dawson. Seven thousand boats left Lake Bennett in the first week after spring thaw in 1898. Since the profitable claims were staked two years earlier, many prospectors left for undiscovered gold elsewhere, settling Alaska in mining camps extending down the Yukon River to Nome.

Jack London and Robert Service

Jack London was a famous and successful writer and political advocate. Raised in the San Francisco Bay area he followed the trail to the Klondike in 1897 at age 21 with many other young Americans looking for gold. He spent just a year in the goldfields and nearly died of starvation and scurvy. But the experience was life altering and formed the basis for his famous novels *The Call of the Wild* and *White Fang* and the short story *To Build a Fire*. Published in 1903 after he returned to California, *The Call of the Wild* is London's most-read book and tells the story of a domesticated dog that becomes a wild animal after serving as a sled dog in the Yukon.

Robert Service was a poet and writer who was born in England and came to the Klondike after the gold rush, living in Dawson City from 1909-12. Service is well regarded throughout Alaska and Canada for popularizing the lore of the Far North. An Anchorage high school is named in his honor. He wrote poems with gold rush themes, including *The Shooting of Dan McGrew* and *The Cremation of Sam McGee,* and he achieved worldwide fame as "the Bard of the Yukon." The first stanza sets the tone for the odd story of the prospector Sam McGee:

> *There are strange things done in the midnight sun*
> *By the men who moil for gold;*
> *The Arctic trails have their secret tales*
> *That would make your blood run cold;*
> *The Northern Lights have seen queer sights,*
> *But the queerest they ever did see*
> *Was that night on the marge of Lake Laberge*
> *I cremated Sam McGee. ...*

Service wrote other poems and short stories on Klondike subjects, including *The Songs of the Sourdough, The Spell of the Yukon, Ballads of a Cheechako, the Trail of Ninety-Eight,* and a novel *The Trail of Ninety-Eight: A Northland Romance*. In 1971 Parks Canada rebuilt his cabin to preserve Klondike Gold Rush structures. Recitations of Service's poetry in the front yard became a popular annual summer tourist attraction.

Nome Goldfields

Many Klondike prospectors continued down the Yukon River to Alaska, searching the interior and coastal regions. In the fall of 1898 gold was discovered in the creeks above Nome. Known as the "Three Lucky Swedes," Jafet Lindeberg, Eric Lindblom, and John Brynteson discovered gold on Anvil and Snow Creeks. News of the strike did not reach the Klondike until the following spring. In a single week, 8,000 people left Dawson for the coast. Thousands more headed north from the Pacific Northwest and California. Like the Klondike, those who came the following spring found all claims staked along all the creeks. Soon placer gold was found in the beach sands at Nome. Since the beach could not be staked, thousands of people mined the sand twenty-four hours a day with gold pans, rockers and sluice boxes. A single nugget was found that weighed over 100 ounces. The beach gave up over $2 million worth of gold that summer.

Many latecomers were jealous of the original discoverers, and tried to "jump" the original claims by filing mining claims covering the same ground. The federal judge ruled the original claims valid, but some of the claim jumpers decided to press their luck, bribing influential politicians. One of them secured the appointment of his crony, Arthur Noyes, as the federal judge for the Nome region, and they conspired to steal the richest claims. The bald-faced theft was eventually stopped when James Wickersham replaced Noyes, but Rex Beach soon wrote about it in his best-selling novel *The Spoilers*, which was made into a stage play, then five times into movies, including one version starring John Wayne and Marlene Dietrich.

Wyatt Earp, the famous lawman, stayed in Nome for a short period. Between 1899 and 1910, miners took more than $46 million worth of gold from the Nome mining district. In the decade after the turn of the century Nome's population reached 20,000 residents. It was the largest city in Alaska with a census of 12,488. But the rush soon collapsed and in 1910 Nome's population had fallen to 2,600. Alaska's largest city was Fairbanks.

The Founding of Fairbanks

At the turn of the century disappointed prospectors roamed the interior of Alaska looking for gold. Merchants were only too happy to oblige by selling gear and supplies for the wanderers. Captain E. T. Barnette founded Fairbanks in August 1901 while trying to set up a trading post upstream from Tanacross, where the Tanana River crossed the established trail from Valdez to Eagle and Dawson. The steamboat ran aground, so prospectors convinced Barnette to set up his trading post where it grounded, seven miles from his destination. At the request of James Wickersham the camp was named after Indiana senator Charles Fairbanks, who later served as Theodore Roosevelt's Vice President.

For several years an Italian immigrant, Felix Pedro, had been searching in the Tanana Hills of the Interior for a gold-rich creek he had found and abandoned years earlier. As the summer of 1901 drew to a close, Pedro found Barnette and purchased enough supplies to keep prospecting. It was a fortunate meeting. Replenished with supplies, on July 22, 1902 Pedro found gold in the nearby Tanana Hills. Pedro was the one who coined the phrase, "There's gold in them there hills."

The Fairbanks Gold Rush, sometimes called the "American Klondike," set off a stampede that transformed the town. By 1908 it was the largest city in Alaska with dozens of saloons in a four-block area. But Pedro did not enjoy his riches for long. He died in Fairbanks of an apparent heart attack eight years later. His partner blamed his wife and years later his body was exhumed and confirmed that Pedro was poisoned.

Alaskaland Park is one of Fairbank's best-known tourist attractions. It opened in 1967 in Fairbanks to commemorate the 100th anniversary of the Alaska purchase. On July 22, 2002, the centennial of Pedro's gold discovery, it was renamed Pioneer Park in his honor. It is home to a permanently docked riverboat *S. S. Nenana*, the Harding rail car, theater, old-time saloon, carousel, three museums, and dozens of gold-rush era cabins.

The gold in the interior is generally buried deep underground. Miners often had to dig 200 feet through permafrost to reach bedrock and find the pay dirt, a difficult process. In time mining technology changed. Miners began using dredges and hydraulic hoses to recover the gold, causing significant environmental damage. Over the years, the total production of the Tanana gold fields was greater than that of other northern gold fields, even the Klondike. The completion of the Alaska Railroad in 1923 cut the cost of freight to the region and helped continue gold mining in the area. The U.S. Smelting, Refining and Mining Company of Massachusetts brought in the first of a fleet of dredges to work the creek beds. In the 1930s, one-third of the population of Fairbanks worked for the mining company.

The Juneau, Nome and Fairbanks gold fields were Alaska's largest, but prospectors found gold in many other places around the territory. Of all the discoveries, the rush to Iditarod in 1909 and 1910 is the best known because of the annual dog sled race that is run over old mail and freight trails that served the area. Large companies took over from individual miners and brought in hydraulic hoses, draglines and small dredges for large-scale placer mining, and built mills at lode mines, but soon the gold played out.

At Ruby Creek discoveries in 1907 and 1910 brought another rush of miners. More than the gold itself, services for miners lead to

Aerial view of a dredge in use along the Farmers Loop Road between College and Fairbanks, 1954. RG 95, Box 6 of 25, Historical Photographs 1906-94, Records of United States Forest Service, Region 10, Juneau. National Archives and Records Administration—Pacific Alaska Region (Anchorage), Picture No. 486914.

the formation of the town and existing residents supplemented their trapping and fishing income by supplying wood for river steamers. In a year Ruby grew from a tent city to a river port. It had running water in summer, a theater, shops and cafés. By 1917, at the height of the rush, creeks south of Ruby yielded $875,000 worth of gold.

Another well-known discovery was made in Valdez. By 1912 over 120 claims were active in the vicinity of Valdez and another 40 near Columbia Glacier to the west. In addition two copper claims were being developed nearby. In all nine stamp mills were in operation in the area employing 250-300 people.

Lode gold deposits in the Willow Creek mining district north of Anchorage were developed in the area of Hatcher Pass. Robert Hatcher discovered gold and staked the first claim in September 1906 and the first lode mill in the area started operating in 1908. Along with all the other gold mines in Alaska, they received a boost in 1933 when President Franklin D. Roosevelt raised the price of gold from $21 an ounce to $35 an ounce. Mines that had not been worked for years reopened, particularly in the interior and Willow mining district, but mining stopped again during World War II by executive order because mines were not essential to the war effort.

After the war, the fixed price of gold at $35 an ounce was not enough to meet the increased cost of labor and to modernize mining equipment. The Independence Mine reopened in 1946 but closed in 1951. In the 1970s the government let the price of gold float and in a few years it soared to $850 an ounce. Mines throughout Alaska reopened and exploration work led to gold discoveries throughout the state.

Historians argue that even more than the fur trade or salmon canning, gold mining changed the Alaska Territory. Despite the industry's aversion to government today, gold mining was the principal reason that government and its infrastructure came to Alaska. After all, gold brought more people to the territory than other industries, founded towns requiring governmental services, and required construction of a telegraph line, trails, roads and the railroad.

Mining in Alaska Today

Nearly all of the large and many of the small placer gold mines currently operating in the Nation are in Alaska. Six modern large-scale hard rock mines operate in Alaska and four produce gold. Recreational mining with gold pans, sluice boxes, rockers and suction dredges is also enjoying resurgence. Much of the government-owned land is open to recreational mining, but most recreational miners operate in the Chugach National Forest and Chugach State Park near Anchorage, as well as at parks on the Kenai Peninsula, the Hatcher Pass area and along the Dalton Highway from Fairbanks to the North Slope.

The opportunity to relive the rich and varied history of Alaska's many gold rushes is available today throughout the state. Many choices are available near Fairbanks. For example, at the El Dorado Gold Mine visitors enjoy a train journey, walking tour and can pan for gold. They also learn the geological history of the region and see fossilized remains of woolly mammoths. Visitors can also pan for gold at the Crow Creek Mine in Girdwood and Denali Park's Kantishna Roadhouse. They can walk through the giant lode operation at Independence Mine State Historical Park near Hatcher Pass and the Klondike Gold Rush National Historical Park at Skagway, which relives the gateway history for the Klondike, including a museum and archives, many reconstructed period buildings and a nearby gold rush cemetery. At Skagway tourists can also take one of Alaska's most popular excursions, the 68 mile White Pass & Yukon Route railway. The railroad was built from 1898 to 1900 and links Skagway with Lake Bennett, climbing 3,000 feet in twenty miles. It features steep grades, cliff-hanging turns and many tunnels, bridges and trestles. Once entering the Yukon, Parks Canada also celebrates the Klondike Gold Rush, with a number of historic opportunities linking Whitehorse, Dawson and the gold fields.

Chapter Six
Territorial Alaska

The tumultuous era of the Klondike Gold Rush changed America's view of the Far North. In 1912 Congress adopted the Second Alaska Organic Act, giving Alaska territorial status, a locally elected legislature and a delegate to Congress. Soon that delegate introduced the first statehood bill. While it took nearly a half-century to achieve statehood, Alaska was finally assured a place in the American conscience.

James Wickersham

James Wickersham was the dominant figure in the century following the Alaska purchase. He was a noted adventurer, federal judge and Alaska advocate. He had never been to Alaska when appointed in 1900 by President William McKinley to take charge of the third judicial district in Eagle City. His circuit included over half the State from coastal Valdez to the Yukon River, in an area of few public buildings and fewer roads. He used revenues from saloon license fees to build courthouses and jails and created Alaska's first legitimate judiciary. His legal decisions are recorded in the seven-volume Alaska Law Reports, among the liveliest and most colorful in American jurisprudence.

Wickersham cleared up the Noyes controversy in Nome soon after his arrival and was later elected Alaska's delegate to Congress, serving from 1908-17 and again during the Depression. As delegate he helped pass the Second Organic Act of 1912, proposed the first Alaska Statehood bill, advanced legislation to establish the Alaska Railroad and helped create the University of Alaska. He also made the first attempt to climb Mt. McKinley in 1903, which was aborted well short of the summit. In his book *Old Yukon: Tails, Trails, and Trial,* he chronicled the expedition and his colorful life as a judge in Alaska.

Territorial Governor John Troy approving the Act creating the University of Alaska on March 12, 1935. Standing from left to right: James Wickersham, Charles Bunnell, Senate President Luther Hess, Reps. Andrew Nerland and A. A. Shonbeck (both members of the Board of Regents), and Speaker of the House J. S. Hofman. Seated: Regent Grace Wickersham, Governor Troy, and Rep. George Lingo, who was both an alumnus and a regent. The university campus in Fairbanks was established in 1917 as the Alaska Agricultural College and School of Mines, first opening for classes in 1922. University of Alaska, General File, UAF-1958-1026-794. Archives, University of Alaska Fairbanks.

Alaska historian Evangeline Atwood, author of *Frontier Politics,* wrote about Wickersham, "No other man has made as deep and varied imprint on Alaska's heritage, whether it be in politics, government, commerce, literature, history or philosophy. A federal judge, member of Congress, attorney and explorer, present-day Alaska is deeply in debt to him." When he retired Wickersham moved to Juneau and purchased a magnificent home overlooking Gastineau Channel. Recognizing the Judge's accomplishments and his collection of historical photographs, artifacts, diaries and scrapbooks, the Alaska Division of Parks and Outdoor Recreation acquired the home in 1984, where the collections and period furnishings are displayed for visitors.

Kennecott Mine

Interior Alaska was alive with prospectors at the turn of the century. In August 1900 Jack Smith and Clarence Warner spotted a green patch of hillside to graze their packhorses during their fruitless search for gold. The green turned out to be a mountain of copper ore, the richest concentration of copper in the world. In 1903 they joined forces with New York's Guggenheim brothers and J.P. Morgan, forming the Kennecott Copper Corporation. The mine was connected underground by a series of tunnels, but the iconic 14 story mill dominated the operation. Ore was hoisted by trams and then hauled by the Copper River and Northwestern Railway 200 miles to Cordova. From there it was shipped to Tacoma for smelting.

The mine operated from 1911-38. There were no environmental or mine remediation laws so when it closed it was simply abandoned, leaving a ghost town. In its 27 years of operation the mine produced a billion tons of ore worth $300,000,000.

Laying steel at Kennecott Mine, 1911; railroad flat cars loaded with supplies. Alaska State Library, Eric A. Hegg Photograph Collection, P124-14.

The dilapidated buildings became a popular tourist destination. After Wrangell-St. Elias National Park was formed, the mine was purchased by the park service. Beginning at the Copper River and ending at the Kennicott River, the McCarthy Road spans 60 miles following the roadbed of the abandoned railway, including the one-lane Kuskulana Bridge and the charming village of McCarthy. Visitors can take a hand tram across the Kennicott River to enjoy this quaint and historically rich area of Alaska.

Salmon Fishery

Commercial fishing for salmon began shortly after the arrival of Europeans on the West Coast. The Hudson's Bay Company shipped salted salmon to the Hawaiian Islands in 1835 and the first salmon cannery opened in 1876. By the turn of the century nearly 100 canneries were in operation in Washington, Oregon and Alaska. While west coast fisheries declined over time they thrived in Southeast and Southcentral Alaska, as well as Bristol Bay. The salmon catch grew with the expansion of cannery capacity through the 1920s. Taxes on every case of salmon contributed 70% of territorial revenues.

The first cannery opened in Bristol Bay in 1883. In a decade millions of cases of salmon were produced annually and salmon packing was Alaska's leading industry. Alaska fishermen worked tirelessly when the summer runs came. They dealt with 20 foot tides, endless mud flats and cold, unpredictable currents. During one treacherous year 136 people drowned. Hundreds of "double ender" sailboats harvested the salmon for half a century until motors were finally allowed in the 1950s.

By the early 1900s the Alaska Packers' Association dominated the salmon harvest. It was formed to sell the surplus pack each year but rose to control the sale of all salmon produced from most of Alaska's canneries. Despite robust harvests and predatory harvest practices, it was an effective lobbyist. So it paid few taxes, blocked fisheries regulations and even resisted statehood. But it also supported its people. In 1919 cannery hospitals provided medical care during the Spanish flu epidemic that devastated western Alaska. While the territorial government was helpless, the Association helped bury the dead and look after orphaned children.

Small wooden salmon sailing fishing boats, called "double enders" because they appear to have two bows, Clarks Point, Bristol Bay, Alaska during 1920s. Alaska State Library, John E. Thwaites Photograph Collection, P18-118.

The Association is also remembered for operating its square-rigger "Star fleet" of tall ships featured on their labels. Although the ships invoked the romance of sail, reliance on wind was a way to save money. Alaska's unpredictable weather caused a number of accidents, most notably the sinking of the *Star of Bengal* in 1908. At the end of the season it left Wrangell with its cannery crew and 2.5 million cans of salmon. A gale blew up and the ship broke apart. Over 100 people died, mostly Chinese and Japanese cannery workers.

In 1916 the Association merged with the California Packing Corporation, reorganized as Del Monte Foods. After World War II, tuna harvests successfully competed with canned salmon so many of the aging plants were closed and Del Monte Foods abandoned the salmon packing business. The Association sold or replaced the square-rigged ships. Two are still on display in San Diego and San Francisco harbors.

The Alaska Railroad

In the era of transcontinental railroads, Alaskans championed construction of a railroad serving Interior Alaska. In 1903 a private line was built 51 miles from Seward to the north. It carried passengers, freight and mail to Turnagain Arm, where the goods were taken by boat at high tide to Matanuska Valley and Interior destinations. When that railroad failed a new owner took over and extended the rails another 21 miles but, like its predecessor, it was forced to close. At the same time a 45 mile

long narrow-gauge line connected the steamship docks in Fairbanks with mining camps. But like their southern cousins, the project was abandoned in 1917. It was clear federal support was necessary so Congress agreed to complete an all-weather 470 mile route from Seward to Fairbanks.

Laying first rails at new U. S. railroad, Ship Creek (Anchorage), ca. 1920. Courtesy of the Library of Congress Prints and Photographs Division, LC-DIG-ppmsc-01808.

In 1914 it bought the bankrupt southern line and moved its headquarters to "Ship Creek," later called "Anchorage," now Alaska's largest city. Three years later it acquired the Tanana Valley Railroad for its terminal facilities, extending its track to Nenana and later converting the track to standard gauge. It then assigned Colonel Frederick Mears, a wartime railroad engineer and decorated hero, to be Chief Engineer of the Alaska Engineering Commission. He enlisted the local Army garrison to settle a labor dispute and then finished the railroad at a cost of $56 million. In 1923 President Warren G. Harding drove the ceremonial golden spike in Nenana. With his job done, Mears left for Seattle to build the Great Northern Railroad Cascade Tunnel under Stevens Pass.

The railroad supported Alaska's growing economy for decades, reaping huge rewards during the buildup of Alaska's defenses before World War II. Along with much of Southcentral Alaska, it suffered catastrophic damage during the 1964 Earthquake. The yards and trackage in Seward, Whittier and along Turnagain Arm were severely damaged but were quickly rebuilt.

President Harding driving in golden spike that completed the Alaska Railroad; Nenana, July 15, 1923. Alaska State Library, Marguerite Bone Wilcox Photograph Collection, P70-85.

In 1985, the State of Alaska bought the railroad for $22.3 million. It then invested $70 million in improvements and repairs that were matched by federal appropriations arranged by Senator Ted Stevens.

The railroad still provides extensive freight and passenger services throughout the "Rail belt" area of the state. There are frequent calls to extend the line, both to connect it to the Canadian prairies, as well as to extend spur lines to Interior Alaska and Point MacKenzie. There are even more fanciful designs to extend the railroad to the Bering Sea, even Siberia, but even Senator Stevens was unable to identify the massive funding required for such schemes.

Snowplow on the Alaska Railroad. UAA-hmc-0381-series2-10-2, Estelle and Philip Garges papers and photographs, Archives and Special Collections, Consortium Library, University of Alaska Anchorage.

The Founding of Anchorage

When Alaska became a territory in 1912, the mouth of Ship Creek was uninhabited. Every other Alaska community was already established, but what is now Alaska's largest city was simply chosen by railroad crews as a convenient anchorage to discharge supplies and set up the railroad headquarters. A tent city of construction workers and suppliers quickly sprang up. The following year lots were auctioned on the bluff above the landing where downtown Anchorage is located today.

Tent houses (Anchorage), ca. 1915. Courtesy of the Library of Congress Prints and Photographs Division, LC-DIG-ppmsc-01745.

Street scene (Anchorage), ca. 1915. Courtesy of the Library of Congress Prints and Photographs Division, LC-DIG-ppmsc-01772.

Anchorage was not formally incorporated until 1920. In its first decade the city's population never exceeded 4,000. After the 1930s air transportation and military defense supplemented the economy. Merrill Field opened in 1930. Elmendorf Air Force Base and Fort Richardson were constructed in the 1940s. The international airport was built in 1951. It was only during the economic boom from World War II that the community became the center of Alaska's population, surpassing the more established Seward, Juneau and Fairbanks.

Sydney Laurence was the first professionally trained artist to make Alaska his home. Born and trained in New York, in 1915 he moved from Valdez to Anchorage and by 1920 was Alaska's most prominent painter. He chose a variety of Alaskan scenes: sailing ships, totem poles, dramatic headlands, cabins under the northern lights and Alaska Natives, miners, and trappers living in the northern wilderness. But his many images of Mt. McKinley from the hills above the Tokositna River became his trademark, which he painted on countless canvases until his death in Anchorage in 1940. He and his wife are buried in the Anchorage Cemetery.

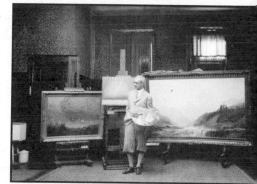

Formal portrait of the artist Sydney Laurence in his Anchorage studio. Two framed paintings and another on an easel. Alaska State Library, Portrait Collection, P01-445.

Like Laurence, Eustace Paul Ziegler loved the Alaska landscape, but he was even more enamored with the people who lived in the challenging environment. His paintings of Native Alaskans, miners, priests, trappers and fishermen are as rugged, independent Alaskans. Ziegler arrived in Cordova in 1909 as a missionary. He moved to Seattle in 1924 but continued to make annual summer trips to the vicinity of Mt. McKinley. In Seattle Ziegler was an influential artist as he continued to paint his favorite themes of Alaska and the rugged people who lived in the northern wilderness.

Fred Machetanz was born in Ohio in 1908 and served as a Naval intelligence officer in the Aleutians. After the war he settled in the Matanuska Valley. His first professional success was writing adventure books, but he soon gained prominence illustrating his wife's books and crafting stone lithographs of sourdough miners, Native Alaskans and dog teams. After a successful exhibition in 1962, Machetanz devoted the rest of his time to painting, usually applying an under painting of white and blue on Masonite. Named Alaskan of the Year in 1977, Machetanz continued to create images of the rugged North until his death in 2002.

Scaling Denali (Mt. McKinley)

Alaska is home to the highest mountain in North America. Though still named Mt. McKinley, most Alaskans prefer its aboriginal name, Denali, "the high one." The mountain is perhaps the single greatest spire in the world because all higher peaks are part of great mountain ranges. McKinley rises almost alone, 16,000 feet above its surroundings. It is also one of the coldest mountains in the world, so its combination of great height, high latitude and terrible weather challenges mountaineers to reach its lofty summit to this day.

The local Koyukon Athabaskan Natives were the first to sight the mountain from the Yukon, Tanana and Kuskokwim river basins. British Captain George Vancouver wrote of "distant stupendous mountains" while in Cook Inlet in 1794. William Dickey, a Seattle prospector panning in the sands of the Susitna River wrote in the late 1890s, "We have no doubt that this peak is the highest in North America and estimate that it is over 20,000 feet high." Dickey named the mountain for William McKinley, a proponent of the gold standard. In 1980 the Alaska Legislature changed its name for the mountain to "Denali."

The first attempt to climb the mountain came in 1903 when Judge James Wickersham failed in his assault on its north face, now called the Wickersham Wall. This route is almost vertical and prone to avalanches so was not successfully climbed until 1963. The famed northern explorer Dr. Frederick Cook claimed the first ascent in 1906 but his claim was disputed and later

View of Mt. McKinley from 20 miles away, Parker-Browne expedition, ca. 1915. Courtesy of the Library of Congress Prints and Photographs Division, LC-DIG-ppmsc-01972.

proved false by the highly regarded Denali photographer and explorer Bradford Washburn. In 1910, four residents of Fairbanks attempted the climb without prior experience. They spent three months getting to and from the mountain and carried a 14 foot spruce pole to the lower North Summit. No one believed the account until the pole was observed three years later. In 1912, the Parker-Browne expedition nearly reached the true summit, but relentless blizzards forced them to abandon the climb a few hundred yards from the top.

Archdeacon Hudson Stuck and Walter Harper at the Allakaket, 1917. Harper was an Alaska Native who on June 7, 1913 was the first person to summit North America's highest peak at age 19. Frederick B. Drane Collection, UAF-1991-46-531, Archives, University of Alaska Fairbanks.

The first ascent of the South Summit came on June 7, 1913 by a party led by Episcopal Archdeacon Hudson Stuck. They ascended the Muldrow Glacier route from the north. The first man to reach the summit was an Alaska Native, 19 year old Walter Harper. Two others joined him, commenting, "The view from the top of Mount McKinley is like looking out the windows of Heaven!" In

1967 Dave Johnston, Art Davidson and Ray Genet completed the first winter ascent, memorialized in Davidson's noteworthy *"Minus 148 Degrees: The First Winter Ascent of Mount McKinley."*

Today the standard climb is the West Buttress route to the south, which starts on a glacier airplane runway at 7,200 feet. Climbers are successful about half the time, usually committing three weeks to reach the summit during April and May. Given the mountain's hostile and ever-changing weather, climbers often spend a week in a tent or snow cave waiting for weather to clear. In the course of hundreds of expeditions there have been infamous failures and dozens have lost their lives. Other routes include the West Rib, a more challenging climb involving a steep snow chute, and the Cassin Ridge, a bone-chilling 50 degree ice and rock climb up the mountain's south face.

Two Mt. McKinley Park buses and one automobile under "Gateway to Mt. McKinley National Park" sign soon after park established in 1920s. Alaska State Library, Skinner Foundation Photograph Collection, P44-05-002.

The summit and much of the terrain to the north became one of America's first national parks in 1917. The impetus was not to protect the mountain but instead the Dall sheep population. After his 1907 visit naturalist Charles Sheldon asked Congress to create a sheep reserve and they instead created Mount McKinley National Park. His account was published posthumously as *The Wilderness of Denali*. The park was expanded in 1980, but inholdings are still found within the park at the traditional hunting and mining camps at Kantishna.

The Nome Serum Run— the "Great Race of Mercy"

In 1925 twenty dog mushers and their teams relayed diphtheria antitoxin nearly 700 miles across Alaska in five and a half days, saving the residents of Nome from a threatening epidemic. The town's only water link to the rest of the world was by steamship and, after the port froze each fall, the 1,000 mile sled dog route was through Iditarod. In late 1924 dozens of local children came down with diphtheria. The needed vaccine came to Nenana on the Alaska Railroad, but delivery required a life saving dog relay to Nome in temperatures reaching -62 °F.

As the mushers progressed more diphtheria cases were reported in Nome. The crisis was headline news and captivated American interest as each day more diphtheria cases were reported as the mushers persevered despite frostbite and hypothermia in the bone-chilling race north. Leonhard Seppala covered the most dangerous leg crossing the frozen Norton Sound in a blizzard. He travelled 200 miles from his home to the

Leonhard Seppala and his dog team. UAA-hmc-0445-series2-1-7, Peter R. and Beulah Marrs Parisi papers, Archives and Special Collections, Consortium Library, University of Alaska Anchorage.

point of rendezvous and then returned with the serum 100 miles toward Nome. He later said "the eddies of drifting, swirling snow passing between the dog's legs and under the bellies made them appear to be fording a fast running river." Gale-force winds drove the wind chill to –70 °F as his lead dog, Togo, led the team in a straight line at night through the raging storm.

Seppala then passed the serum to Gunnar Kaasen, whose lead dog Balto led all the way to Nome in whiteout conditions so extreme that Kaasen could not see the dogs that were harnessed closest to his sled. Although there had been many deaths from diphtheria that winter, the fresh serum stemmed the tide. Forty-three new cases were later diagnosed but they were treated with the fresh supply of antitoxin.

America's response to the heroic journey was overwhelming. Each musher received a letter of commendation from President Coolidge, a gold medal, a cash prize and the

Postcard, "A crack dog team, Alaska," ca. 1890. Box 279, Donated Materials in the National Archives, Henry S. Wellcome Collection, 1856-1936. National Archives and Records Administration—Pacific Alaska Region (Anchorage), ARC Record 297825.

U.S. Senate recessed to recognize the event. Mushers and their teams even toured the country and starred in a 30 minute film *"Balto's Race to Nome."* A statue of Balto was unveiled in New York's Central Park. Seppala was upset when the media attributed Togo's achievements to Balto, but the media ignored the Native mushers who covered two-thirds the distance to Nome.

Interest in dog sledding declined when the use of snowmachines spread throughout Alaska in the 1960s. But mushing was soon revitalized as a recreational sport. In 1975 Dorothy Page and Joe Redington founded the Iditarod Trail Sled Dog Race, the "Last Great Race on Earth." The legendary race, which runs each year 1,150 miles from Anchorage to Nome, has many traditions that commemorate the Nome Serum Run and particularly the daring exploits of Leonhard Seppala and his lead dog Togo.

Bush Pilots in Alaska

First airplane in operation in the Nome & Seward Peninsula area, 1927, piloted by the famous bush pilot Noel Wien. Edward Lewis Bartlett Papers, UAF-1969-95-536, Archives, University of Alaska Fairbanks.

The exploration and settlement of Alaska exploded with the development of aircraft. Although unfavorable weather still makes flying a dangerous occupation, the mystique of the Alaska "bush pilot" pervades Alaska's twentieth century history. The first bush pilot was Carl Ben Eielson, who learned to fly during World War I and came to Alaska to teach and fly. He won an airmail contract between Fairbanks and McGrath. Later he flew the breadth of the state. He was the first pilot across the Arctic Ocean, reaching Spitzbergen 2,200 miles from Barrow in 20 hours, then charted unknown islands in Antarctica. In November 1929 he died in a crash in Siberia while rescuing a stranded cargo vessel. His name was given to an Air Force base and a university building in Fairbanks, as well as a visitor center in Denali National Park.

Noel Wien was another pioneer aviator who migrated to Alaska with his brothers to learn to fly. A legend among legendary pilots, Wien had just 500 hours of stunt flying experience when he arrived in the state. He went on to become Alaska's most gifted pilot, operating a flying service on the Seward Peninsula and founding a major airline.

Bristol Bay Air Service float planes. UAA-hmc-0445-series2-1-59, Peter R. and Beulah Marrs Parisi papers, Archives and Special Collections, Consortium Library, University of Alaska Anchorage.

He was also the first to fly from Fairbanks to Seattle and Fairbanks to Nome, as well as to make a round-trip flight between Alaska and Asia.

Don Sheldon was a highly regarded glacier pilot who operated Talkeetna Air Service for decades. He ferried climbers, hunters and fishermen to inaccessible places in the Alaska Interior, but was best known for his daring rescues of climbers on Denali and pioneering the technique of glacier landings until his untimely death in 1975. Many other pilots support mountain climbers to this day, but Sheldon's exploits were both new and unique. His 1974 biography, *"Wager with the Wind: the Don Sheldon Story,"* chronicles his adventures.

The Matanuska Colony

The Depression forced dramatic changes in Alaska. Prices for fish and copper produced in the state plummeted, while the supply of commodities shipped to Alaska grew. Wages declined and the workforce decreased by half. Using his "New Deal" policies to bolster the economy, President Franklin D. Roosevelt decided to relocate hundreds of Midwesterners from Michigan, Minnesota and Wisconsin to resettle in Alaska's Matanuska Valley.

Colony Farmers & Trading Post Palmer, Alaska [ca. 1936-1937]. UAA-hmc-421-series 2-2, Ruby I. Cashen papers, Archives and Special Collections, Consortium Library, University of Alaska Anchorage.

A year after the project was announced, the first contingent arrived at Palmer in 1935. The government agreed to give each farmer 40 acre tracts, as well as a modest home and barn. The colonists struggled with a short growing season, high freight prices, high labor costs and distant markets. It was a constant challenge until nearby military jobs became available during the war. While the project gave Alaska a national profile, the experiment did not live up to the initial excitement. By 1959 only ten percent of the original 200 families were still farming.

Despite further efforts by the state to harness the potential for barley and dairy farming in the decades after Statehood, agriculture in Alaska continues along the margins to the modern day. But each year the Alaska State Fair features the wonders of Alaska farming, with contests among giant, fertilizer-enhanced cabbages, zucchinis, turnips, radishes and pumpkins. The secret for success is kept confidential by the competitors, but vigilant care and endless daylight contributes to the size of the biggest vegetables.

Chapter Seven
Alaska at War

*A*laska is the only U.S. territory that has been occupied by a foreign power in the last two centuries. In 1942 the Japanese Empire overran the islands of Attu and Kiska and bombed U.S. military installations at Dutch Harbor. It was the only occupation of America during World War II. Historians continue to debate the reason Japanese commanders set their sights on Alaska, particularly the remote and windswept Aleutian Islands, but the decision ended Alaska's traditional isolation and at once it became the strategic centerpiece of America's defense that continues to this day.

Alaska Prepares for World War II

Alaska and the Aleutian Islands are strategically situated in the center of the "Great Circle" airline route from North America to Asia. In 1935 General Billy Mitchell alerted Congress, stating, "I believe that in the future, whoever holds Alaska will hold the world. I think it is the most important strategic place in the world." The Japanese Empire likewise focused on this importance, reasoning that control of the Aleutians would not only give them an advantage attacking the West Coast, but also prevent a possible U.S. counterattack.

By 1940 the U.S. began to build its military to protect ports and strategic locations from the Japanese, but they focused on Pearl Harbor, the Philippines and the Marshall Islands. At the time Alaska had a population of just 72,500 people. And many urged that Alaska be included in this build-up. Residents also saw the economic advantage if the military were to commit resources to the State. This advocacy, coupled with Japan's growing belligerence, finally prompted the government to respond. The War Department built naval air, destroyer and submarine bases in Sitka, Kodiak, and Dutch Harbor in 1939 and 1940. The Army established forts and airfields at Anchorage and Fairbanks and an aircraft cold weather testing station (later Ladd Field) in Fairbanks.

In order to assure supply of these military installations, especially if Japan blocked coastal shipping, the U.S. built a series of airfields from Montana north through Canada to Fairbanks. To further link these Alaskan outposts, the Army punched the Alcan Highway through Canadian and Alaskan wilderness from northern Alberta to connect with the Richardson Highway at Delta. From Glennallen a spur road (the present-day Glenn Highway) was built to connect Anchorage to the Alcan Highway via the existing Richardson Highway. Despite these preparations there were fewer than 300 soldiers in Alaska in 1940. All of them were stationed at Chilkoot Barracks near Haines, an unlikely place to respond to a Japanese attack. This soon changed. By the outbreak of World War II in late 1941 Alaska's military population swelled to 35,000, and in another year it exceeded 100,000. The civilian population also grew as contractors found a robust economy near the military posts. Military defense capabilities continue to support the Alaska economy to this day.

The Japanese never mounted a threat to mainland Alaska or American coastal shipping, but the airfields served a significant role even after hostilities ceased in Alaska later in the war. Beginning in 1943 the Air Transport Command ferried nearly 8,000 fighters and bombers from U.S. production plants via the Alaska Highway, Fairbanks and Nome to the Soviet Union for attacks against Nazi Germany. Many of the pilots were women who were organized as the Women's Army Corps to fly lend-lease aircraft to Ladd Field near Fairbanks. In Fairbanks Soviet pilots collected the aircraft and flew them westward to Europe.

Japanese Occupation of Alaska

In 1941 the Japanese military decided to strike in a surprise attack against America's Pacific installations. The first crippling blow came with the bombing of Pearl Harbor, which was followed by the invasion of Alaska six months later. At the time it was widely believed the Aleutian campaign was a diversion intended to draw out the U.S. Pacific Fleet during the naval Battle of Midway since the same Japanese commander launched them. But historians today believe the Japanese invaded the Aleutians to protect the empire's northern flank. Nonetheless during a few short weeks in 1942 Attu and Kiska Islands were invaded and the naval installations at Dutch Harbor were bombed.

Japanese Attack on Dutch Harbor, June 3, 1942. Group of Marines on the alert between attacks. Smoke from burning fuel tanks in background set afire from a Japanese dive bomber the previous day. Item from Record Group 80: General Records of the Department of the Navy, 1804 - 1983. National Archives and Records Administration, Still Picture Records Section, Special Media Archives Services Division, College Park, MD. ARC ID 520589 / Local Identifler 80-G-12076.

Whittier Tunnel, ca. 1955. RG 77, Box 32, Construction Project Photographs 1950-85, Records of the Office of the Chief of Engineers, U. S. Army Corps of Engineers, Alaska District (Anchorage). National Archives and Records Administration—Pacific Alaska Region (Anchorage), ARC ID 5150368, Photos 96-430IN.

In the panic that followed the invasion martial law was imposed and many Aleuts relocated from their homelands near the front. Allied commanders geared for war assuming the Japanese would use the Aleutians as a base to attack the Pacific Northwest. The Japanese carefully mapped the Alaska

Coast before the war so people up and down the coast expected a broad scale assault at any moment.

The American military sent thousands of personnel to Alaska to such places as Fort Richardson and Eielson Air Force Base. Runways were constructed in Northway and Sitka. Mark Field was built in Nome. The U.S. Army built Whittier as a port, hollowing a 3 mile tunnel from rock. Fortifications were constructed in Kodiak, Seward and other coastal sites. Fort Greely was established as an armed forces cold weather proving ground.

The Battles of Attu and Kiska

It took nearly a year to eject the Japanese from Attu and Kiska. In the first months of the occupation the Americans pounded Japanese positions with airstrikes. But the remoteness of the islands and the difficulties of climate and terrain prevented effective bombing. More American

Attu, Aleutian Islands. Landing boats pouring soldiers and their equipment onto the beach at Massacre Bay. This is the Southern landing force. Courtesy of the Library of Congress Prints and Photographs Division, LC-USW33-032360-C.

aircraft were lost in the violent gales and low visibility than by enemy fire. Recognizing the futility of this strategy a new campaign was adopted. The Americans had to first isolate the Japanese from their regular supplies and then attack each island in turn. It was a brutal, miserable and grievous campaign, regarded as among the worst in the war due to both the hostile weather and fierce enemy combat.

The Battle of the Commander Islands began in March 1943 as Navy ships intercepted and turned back a Japanese flotilla attempting to bring reinforcements, isolating the Aleutian invaders. Then 15,000 American troops waded ashore at Attu in May 1943 and after two and half weeks defeated the 2,400 Japanese defenders. The Japanese defenders did not contest the landings but rather dug in on high ground away from the shore.

At first a shortage of landing craft, unsuitable beaches, and inadequate equipment made the American attack ineffectual. Soldiers then suffered from frostbite because essential supplies could not be landed or could not be moved to needed locations.

American soldiers launching the attack on Attu Ridge in May 1943. By the end of the month the battle of Attu ended with American victory and the Japanese occupiers driven from American soil. Alaska State Library, U.S. Army. 172nd Infantry Brigade Photograph Collection, P08-34.

Once the Americans were ashore, violent fighting ensued. When the battle was nearly over a Japanese force suddenly attacked near Massacre Bay in a relentless banzai charge. The battle penetrated to the shocked rear-echelon units of the American force, nearly cutting their lines in two. After a vicious close-quarter counter-attack, the Japanese were killed to the last man.

Japanese prisoners at Attu. Only a few Japanese prisoners were captured during the fighting at Massacre Bay. Most were killed in the fierce fighting or committed suicide to avoid capture. Alaska State Library, U.S. Army. 172nd Infantry Brigade Photograph Collection, P08-35.

Only 28 prisoners were taken, none of them an officer. U.S. burial teams counted 2,351 Japanese dead though hundreds more were probably obliterated by bombardments over the course of the battle. The U.S. suffered nearly 4,000 casualties (580 killed in battle, 1,148 battlefield injuries, 1,200 weather-related injuries, 614 from disease, and 318 other deaths from friendly fire and booby traps exploding after hostilities ceased).

Kiska landing 1943. American and Canadian troops had by-passed the island of Kiska as they pressed on to Attu Island where the decisive action of the war in the Aleutians took place. Returning to take Kiska after the Battle of Attu they found that the Japanese forces had evacuated the island under the cover of fog. Alaska State Library, U.S. Army. 172nd Infantry Brigade Photograph Collection, P08-36.

Recognizing the difficulties at Attu the American command assembled an even larger force to invade Kiska. But in late July the Japanese managed a brilliant escape when eight ships dashed to Kiska and carried away the emperor's soldiers undetected. American bombers hit abandoned positions for almost three weeks when an American and Canadian force invaded what proved to be a deserted island.

The Battle for the Aleutians is known as the "Forgotten Battle" since it was overshadowed by the near simultaneous Guadalcanal campaign that ended in early 1943. Nonetheless, by August 1943 the Japanese were removed from Alaska. Although the Americans planned to invade northern Japan from Adak, the plans were not

Official U.S. Navy photograph of American attack on Japanese base at Kiska, June 1942. Alaska State Library, Aleutian/Pribilof Project Photograph Collection, P233-V109.

executed. Instead over 1,500 missions were flown against the Kurile Islands, diverting 500 Japanese planes and 41,000 ground troops from the larger battlefields of the South Pacific.

Castner's Cutthroats

One of the most celebrated if not irregular commands of World War II was the army unit established to weather the difficult conditions of the Aleutian terrain. The brainchild of Col. Lawrence V. Castner, an Army intelligence officer serving in the Alaskan Defense Command, "Castner's Cutthroats" were organized to live off the land with only minimal outfitting to reconnoiter and when necessary strike at Japanese positions while they occupied Attu and Kiska. Hard and dangerous men, they often had colorful nicknames like "Bad Whiskey Red," "Aleut Pete" and "Waterbucket Ben."

Castner chose men who thrived in the tough conditions of the Alaskan wilderness, including many Alaska Natives, and used modest watercraft (kayaks and canoes) to move from island to island without observation. They were permitted their own weapons rather than standard Army issue and lived off the land, frequently stopping so they could subsist for long periods in the field. Trapper Nelson packs, which held all their supplies for their mountainous treks, were standard issue.

Castner's Cutthroats was integral to Alaska's defense by conducting reconnaissance missions. They also helped plan landing zones for American amphibious assaults to retake the islands. One of their greatest achievements was to build an airfield on Adak Island near Attu. The army lost many planes due to Alaska weather so the Cutthroats built an airfield on Adak, damming and draining a lagoon so its sandy bottom could be used as a temporary landing strip. During the seizure of Attu the Cutthroats served as guides and messengers for the army regulars. Many soldiers owe their lives to the Cutthroats for protecting them from the weather and providing them with food.

The Alaska Territorial Guard

The Alaska Territorial Guard (ATG) was formed to stand watch over Alaska's lengthy coastline. Established before the war, the majority of guard members were Alaska Natives who became the "eyes and ears" of the Arctic and served the country without pay. They were considered to be the "unorganized militia" and separate from the National Guard, which was the "organized militia."

After hostilities broke out in 1941 the few regular troops were sent out of Alaska for active duty on other fronts. Territorial Governor Ernest Gruening quickly moved to expand the ATG with accelerated recruitment in towns and villages throughout the territory. Alaska Native men, raised as hunters, knew the terrain and weather intimately and could live off the land, so were crucial to the ATG.

When they were enlisted the Guardsmen were provided little beyond a rifle, ammunition, and an identification patch for their clothing. A local officer was appointed and instructions given about what to do if the Japanese invaded. Although they did not come into contact with the Japanese, the establishment of the ATG, which became the National Guard after the war, was important to many rural communities. Many men and later many women joined the ATG and were sent for training outside their villages, which for some was the first time they had traveled any distance from their homes or earned money. The ATG became one of the forces that changed Alaska Native life after the war.

Aleut Relocation

When the Japanese struck Alaska in June 1942, Japanese aircraft bombed Dutch Harbor and troops occupied the western most Aleutian Islands. A small naval party on Kiska and Aleut villagers on Attu were taken prisoner and transported to Japan where they were held until the end of the war. Concerned that the war would come to other far western islands that could not be defended, the Army evacuated 881 residents from the Aleutian Islands west of Unimak Island and all the residents of the Pribilof Islands. They also destroyed many of the vacated island homes rather than let the invaders use them.

The evacuees had little time to prepare and could pack only one bag before boarding a troop ship to sail away. Most had never left home let alone understood the reasons for the war or the forced evacuation. They were not told how long they would be gone or even where they were going. It would be nearly four years before they returned and for most it would never be the same.

The Aleuts were relocated to five isolated camps throughout Southeast Alaska, 1,500 miles away in a strange rain forest land that suffocated Native people accustomed to treeless windswept tundra. There they were left to suffer from neglect, malnutrition and disease. The most deplorable conditions were at Funter Bay on Admiralty Island, but other camps included an old gold mine and an equally dilapidated abandoned cannery. With light pouring in between cracks and people falling through dry rotted floors, these places were vermin-ridden and incapable of being heated. Survivors speak of constantly being cold, hungry and sick.

An estimated one in 10 died in the camps, a death rate not far behind the percentage of American soldiers who perished in prisoner of war camps. Those who survived returned home to find their houses and churches ransacked and destroyed, in many cases by their own country's military forces. In 1988 Congress paid modest reparations to the few Aleuts and larger number of Japanese-Americans for the consequences of their forced relocation during the war.

Construction of the Alaska Highway

Proposals for a highway from the lower 48 states to Alaska originated in the 1920s when Alaskans and Canadians urged construction of an international highway connecting the United States, Canada and Russia. In order to promote the highway a wily Alaskan, Slim Williams, travelled the proposed route by dog sled then later by motorcycle. But the project suffered from lack of interest. The Canadian Parliament saw no value in advancing construction funds for the road since only a few thousand residents of the Yukon Territory would benefit.

But the attack on Pearl Harbor and the Aleutians changed all that and in February 1942 Congress and President Roosevelt approved the construction of the Alcan Highway, often called the Alaska Highway in the U.S. Canada was in full agreement but only with the understanding the United States would pay the cost of construction and that the parts of the road within Canada would be turned over to local authority after the war.

Construction started on March 8, 1942 when hundreds of pieces of construction equipment were assembled by train in Dawson Creek, British Columbia, now Milepost "0" of the Alaska Highway. The project accelerated after the spring thaw when crews were able to work from both the northern and southern ends. An estimated 11,500 GIs labored on the project for 12 and 16 hour days. Another 7,500 civilians worked for the generous wage of $1/hour.

Soldiers of the 95th General Services Regiment working on the Alaska Highway, Sikanni Chief River Bridge, British Columbia. NWCS/H. Reed., National Archives and Records Administration, College Park, MD. Photo No. 111-SC-139940.

The all-Black 93rd, 95th and 97th Army Engineer General Service Regiments of the Corps of Engineers built the Alaska portion of the road, its most difficult and hazardous section. Initially opposed by the Alaska Command due to segregation policies, these African American regiments served in bitter cold to help complete the project in eight months and 12 days at a cost of just $135 million. To expedite construction, the Army commandeered private property along the route, including local riverboats, railway locomotives and housing originally destined for California.

On September 24, 1942 crews from both directions met at Mile 588 at Contact Creek near the British Columbia-Yukon border. The twisting 1,400 mile highway was dedicated and opened for military traffic on November 20, 1942 at Soldiers Summit. During the first winter a series of truck convoys carried supplies in frigid conditions to support U.S. forces in the Aleutians and lend-lease equipment for Soviet Russia.

Although the project was announced as "complete" it was not usable by general vehicles for another year. There were steep grades, muddy surfaces from exposed permafrost, numerous switchbacks and almost no protective guardrails. Pontoon bridges used to temporarily open the road in 1942 were replaced with logs, then steel. Nonetheless, road construction in such a short time frame was a considerable engineering achievement binding the Far North to the rest of the Nation, sustaining Alaska's military installations from the threat of invasion.

The War's Aftermath

Following the war the Alaska Territorial Guard units were transferred into the National Guard and armories were constructed in the larger Native villages, where most of the adult male population and later many of the women enlisted. Native guard members were also provided with training in Anchorage or other military bases, exposing many of them for the first time to an urban environment. At the same time the U.S. military was an early proponent of desegregation, which helped break down prejudice against Alaska Natives in the non-Native population.

On April 1, 1946 the U.S. Army transferred control of the Canadian portion of the Alcan Highway to the Yukon and British Columbia governments, where it has served as a lifeline and tourism destination for residents of northern British Columbia, the Yukon Territory and the Alaskan Interior ever since. The road opened to the public in 1948 and the Alaska section was paved during the 1960s. The road was improved and straightened over the years such that the historic milepost markings are no longer accurate. The Canadian portion was paved during the 1990s. Now called the Alaska Highway, it remains an important roadway and tourist adventure to this day, hosting nearly 100,000 travelers each year. The modern road snakes peacefully from British Columbia grain fields and aspen groves through Yukon's historic gold fields to the black spruce forests of Interior Alaska.

The war had other unintended consequences that shaped the future of Alaska. Service personnel stationed in Alaska during the war learned that the stereotype of Alaska as a land of ice and igloos was false and instead discovered that Alaska was a desirable place to live. Many of the people who became key players in Alaska's history, such as Governor Jay Hammond (1974-1982), were war veterans who made Alaska their home.

A former military station in Sitka became Mt. Edgecumbe High School. It was opened in 1947 by the Bureau of Indian Affairs as a boarding school for rural Native high school students and now operates with funds from the State of Alaska. Many Mt. Edgecumbe graduates became leaders of Alaska Native communities and played a key role in the battle for Statehood and Alaska Native land claims in the decades that followed.

The Cold War

Early warning. Clear, Alaska. U. S. Army Air Force photo. UAA-hmc-0370-series15b-30-4, Christine M. McClain papers, Archives and Special Collections, Consortium Library, University of Alaska Anchorage.

Soon after World War II concluded, a new kind of war began with the Soviet Union, Alaska's neighbor across the Bering Sea. The Soviets perfected intercontinental ballistic missile technology in the 1950s and so the United States required the construction of a network of "distant early warning" air defense radar and communications facilities to warn of any surprise attack from Soviet bombers or missiles. Because of the limitations of electronic equipment at the time these stations were usually constructed in isolated sites throughout

Alaska and northern Canada to maximize the radar's capacity to detect enemy incursions. Each base required a number of personnel and a supply network to maintain the complex electronics of the day.

Tatalina Aircraft Control & Warning System Radome and White Alice Site, 1958, Upper Camp. RG 77, Box 30, Construction Project Photographs 1950-85, Records of the Office of the Chief of Engineers, U. S. Army Corps of Engineers, Alaska District (Anchorage). National Archives and Records Administration—Pacific Alaska Region (Anchorage), ARC ID 5150368, Photos 96-397IN.

These defense systems were all linked together for decades in a cohesive network of 84 stations called "White Alice," connected in turn to an integrated defense network, the North American Air Defense Command (NORAD), located in Colorado. America's defense was dependent upon Alaska for advance warning and initial interception. NORAD said the system of early warning detection would give the lower 48 states a 15 minute warning in the event of a Soviet missile attack.

In the 1970s satellite communications replaced the White Alice system, although a few of the sites remain active as part of a radar modernization program. Given Alaska's strategic geographic location in relation to Russia and other Asian trouble spots, a significant number of Army, Air Force and other personnel continue be to stationed at military installations throughout Alaska to this day.

Tatalina Aircraft Control & Warning System, 1958, AFS. RG 77, Box 30, Construction Project Photographs 1950-85, Records of the Office of the Chief of Engineers, U. S. Army Corps of Engineers, Alaska District (Anchorage). National Archives and Records Administration—Pacific Alaska Region (Anchorage), ARC ID 5150368, Photos 96-3984IN.

Chapter Eight
The Fight for Statehood

After the adoption of the Second Organic Act in 1912 there was a semblance of self-government in Alaska but outsiders still wielded substantial influence over the decisions that affected everyday lives in the territory. James Wickersham urged statehood but national leaders believed that Alaska's population was too small, the economy was too fragile and the location was too distant to merit statehood. So second-class territorial status continued for a half century.

It was only after America discovered Alaska's strategic importance in World War II that Ernest Gruening, Bob Bartlett, Bob Atwood and Bill Egan achieved what was previously unthinkable. President Eisenhower signed the bill to admit Alaska as the 49th state on July 7, 1958. Six months later, on January 3, 1959, it was admitted into the Union.

Alaska as Territory

In the early days of America, before the U.S. constitution was adopted, the Northwest Ordinance of 1787 set the framework for administering newly acquired possessions like the Louisiana Purchase and the Oregon Country. Each remained a territory until migration and free enterprise enabled the area to sustain itself economically. It was then admitted to the Union as a state. Some of the territories had lengthy waits; others were quickly admitted.

The non-contiguous territories, particularly Alaska, were treated differently. Because of the controversy about its acquisition, Congress failed to provide any civil government in Alaska for almost two decades. There were a few Army and Customs personnel offering some protection in Sitka and other outposts, but the colony was otherwise lawless. In 1884 the Alaska Organic Act gave Alaska a few judges, clerks, marshals and other government officials, but most decisions were still made outside the region.

Fishing, trapping, mining and mineral production were soon underway as Americans poured into the Far North for a fresh start. But the resources were depleted without recourse because powerful financial interests prevented self-governance. In 1906 the Guggenheim brothers and J. P. Morgan formed the "Alaska Syndicate" to operate the Kennecott copper mine and steamship companies. The Alaska Packers' Association took control of the salmon harvest. Neither exercised any self-control and lobbied successfully against regulation.

James Wickersham was particularly concerned about this exploitation and undertook a personal fight for Alaskan self-rule. He took advantage of a controversy that gripped the Nation in 1909, the Ballinger-Pinchot Affair. President Taft appointed the former mayor of Seattle to be Secretary of Interior who became mired with the Alaska Syndicate in plans to develop Alaska coalfields and forestlands to their mutual advantage. While he was eventually exonerated, the controversy swayed the President to support Wickersham's pleas for home rule.

In 1912, the year Arizona and New Mexico were admitted to the Union, Congress passed the Second Organic Act. The law finally named Alaska as a U.S. territory with a governor appointed by the President. This gave both men and women the right to elect a two-house legislature. But the federal bureaucracy retained control over fishing, hunting and natural resource extraction. Alaska was also granted the right to elect a non-voting delegate to Congress. Wickersham was promptly elected Alaska's Delegate and, in four years, offered the first statehood bill. But there was no enthusiasm for statehood, even among Alaskans. President Harding sensed this disinterest when he made his grand tour of the territory in 1923.

Ernest Gruening and Bob Bartlett

Despite territorial status, the absentee financial interests continued to dominate resource decisions and efforts to expand home rule were repelled. Congress went so far as to adopt the Jones Act and the White Act, sponsored by a Seattle Congressman, to give outside interests greater control over Alaska's resources, particularly its fisheries. These laws required that Alaska be served by U.S. maritime carriers and authorized fish traps, a particularly efficient salmon harvest practice.

When the Alaska economy collapsed during the Depression, President Roosevelt took two actions that changed the course of Alaska history. First, he gave attention to Alaska's economic potential by relocating midwesterners to the Matanuska Valley Colony and, second, he appointed Ernest Gruening Governor of Alaska.

The war years also changed Alaska. In 1940 fewer than 1,000 of Alaska's 72,500 residents were military. By 1943 over half (152,000 of 233,000) were part of the armed forces. Although there was a brief decline after the war, Cold War military expenditures pushed the population to 128,000 by 1950. During this transformation a number of discharged veterans settled in the state. Moving from other states, they saw no reason why Alaskans should not have the same power as a state to govern themselves as their home states. Like long-time residents, they also resented federal bureaucrats who applied rules and regulations that did not fit Alaska's unsettled and undeveloped conditions.

Territorial government and tax structures also seemed to favor outside interests such as the Alaska Steamship Company, which enjoyed an effective monopoly on steamship travel. Even Alaskan businessmen like the Lomen brothers of Nome and Austin E. "Cap" Lathrop of Anchorage argued against statehood because they did not pay appreciable local taxes. It was not long before the national press became aware of this stranglehold. In a telling article, *Newsweek* said Alaska was gripped in a "feudal barony" where the absentee-owned mining and fishing corporations took out millions in natural resources and left next to nothing behind in the form of social and economic benefits--a "looted land."

Ernest Gruening, a Harvard-trained doctor with a history of progressive politics, served as editor of the *Nation* until he was appointed by President Roosevelt as governor in 1939. He served until 1953. Upon arrival he learned that Alaska was still without adequate roads, air-fields, hospitals, health care and dependable shipping at reasonable cost. Further, the aboriginal rights issue had not yet been settled so homesteaders were hard-pressed to acquire land from the federal government. Soon he was at odds with the outside salmon, shipping and mining indus-tries. He wanted to implement new taxes but found the current tax system favored the special interests. He later wrote, "The wealth of Alaska was being drained off and next to nothing was staying there for its needs." He spent the next ten years fighting for enough revenues to support a worthy government, concluding that statehood was nec-essary to protect Alaska from outside interests.

Edward Lewis "Bob" Bartlett served as secretary to Alaska's Congressional delegate Anthony J. Dimond. He was the federal official to cut the ribbon when the Alcan Highway was completed in 1943. Later that year he was back gold min-ing in Alaska when he was elected the Territorial Delegate to Congress, the same position previously held by Wickersham and Dimond. Beginning in 1944 Gruening and Bartlett joined together in their 15 year campaign for Alaska and its state-hood entitlement. After the war most members of Congress opposed statehood. The Japanese invasion and Cold War highlighted Alaska's strategic importance, but statehood was deferred because of Alaska's modest population and unstable economy. But Gruening and Bartlett were not deterred. In 1946 they launched a statehood referendum, which passed by a three to two margin. The results showed that Alaskans sup-ported statehood. So Bartlett introduced his first statehood bill in Congress. It was tabled. Republicans feared that Alaska could not raise enough taxes to sustain itself and Southern Democrats were afraid that Alaska, a traditionally Democratic state, would elect pro-civil rights congressmen.

Gruening and Bartlett kept pressing, asking the territorial legislature to establish the "Alaska Statehood Committee," which was chaired by the owner and publisher of the *Anchorage Times*, Robert "Bob" Atwood. Atwood, who came to Alaska in 1935, was a tireless statehood advocate who wrote frequently of his statehood dreams in the state's largest circulation newspaper. Using Gruening's East Coast connections, the Committee enlisted journalists, newspaper editors, state governors and labor organizations to educate and advocate Alaskan statehood. Prominent Americans such as Eleanor Roosevelt, actor James Cagney, author Pearl Buck, journalist John Gunther, historian Arthur Schlesinger, Jr. and theologian and commentator Reinhold Niebuhr were soon enlisted. Even President Truman supported statehood.

In addition to stimulating the interest of American leaders, thousands of regular Alaskans were enlisted to write relatives and friends throughout the country to generate popular interest in the statehood drive. The *New York Journal-American* put the situation dramatically: "Alaska wants statehood with the fervor men and women give to a transcendent cause. An overwhelming number of men and women voters in the United States want statehood for Alaska. This Nation needs Alaskan statehood to advance her defense, sustain her security and discharge her deep moral obligation."

With such emotional and enthusiastic support Bartlett introduced another bill in 1949. It passed the House by a slim margin. The Southern Democrats threatened a filibuster in the Senate, so the bill died. The Korean War put concerns about Alaska statehood on the back burner but in 1954 President Eisenhower inadvertently rekindled it. In his State of the Union address that year the Republican President spoke in favor of statehood, but for Hawaii (then a Republican state) but not Alaska (then a Democratic state). This blunder emboldened Gruening, Bartlett and other statehood advocates in both territories. A Senate coalition quickly formed that tied the fate of Alaska and Hawaii together. They argued if both states were admitted together any perceived political leanings would cancel. Hawaii was admitted as a state eight months after Alaska.

Eisenhower's gaffe also compelled the Senate Interior and Insular Affairs Committee to travel to the two states to learn local sentiments. The response in Alaska was overwhelming. Margaret Rutledge of Anchorage was one of hundreds to speak when the committee came to Alaska. She was outraged that Alaskans went through immigration screening at the Seattle airport, a process usually reserved for foreign nationals. She ended her testimony in tears, complaining this "degrading influence had robbed me of the thing I valued most, my birthright as an American."

"Operation Statehood" was underway. The Alaska Statehood Committee rallied residents all over the state to the cause. They sent pro-statehood Christmas cards to friends and relatives that read, "Make [Alaskans] future bright/Ask your Senator for statehood/And start the New Year right." The Committee also sent bouquets of Alaska's flower, the Forget Me-Not, to members of Congress. "Lack of public interest" was no longer a valid excuse.

The Constitutional Convention and the Tennessee Plan

In 1955 the territorial legislature convened a constitutional convention to write a state constitution suitable for Congressional approval. The model was America's own constitution, which was framed by a 55 member Philadelphia convention in 1787. So a Constitutional Convention of 55 elected delegates (49 men and six women, including one Alaska Native) met at Constitution Hall on the campus of the University of Alaska, Fairbanks. Popular grocer and former Valdez mayor, William A. "Bill" Egan, chaired the convention. Egan represented Valdez in the territorial House of Representatives from 1940 to 1953. He was then elected to the territorial Senate. Never a pretentious man, he arrived in Fairbanks for the convention by hitching a ride on a truck from Valdez.

The convention received extensive national exposure and was praised by journalists and news commen-

Constitutional Convention with Convention President and later Governor Bill Egan seated facing convention, 1955-56, William A. Egan Papers, UAF-1985-120-259, Archives, University of Alaska Fairbanks.

tators for its non-partisan attention to "the good of Alaska." It was an emotional event, as passions about the future of Alaska ran among convention members. Bartlett, Atwood and Gruening attended the convention and Gruening gave a stirring speech that compared Alaska's status to the American struggle for independence. His speech was entitled "Let Us End American Colonialism" and it reached far into the National conscience. Even the university's student body president urged the delegates and Americans to support the crusade for statehood.

The delegates met for 75 days and wrote a model constitution praised to this day. It was based on a National Municipal League model and the recently adopted constitutions of Missouri, New Jersey and Hawaii. Although less verbose than other state constitutions, 14,400 words, the focus was to repair weaknesses in current resource management and territorial administration. Delegates were also careful to protect individual citizens' rights and adopt safeguards against inefficient and partisan government. The delegates adopted the constitution with a single opponent on February 5, 1956. Alaskans then overwhelmingly approved it on April 24, 1956. The constitution became effective on January 3, 1959 when Alaska was admitted to the Union.

In the 1956 election Alaska voters also adopted the "Tennessee Plan" to elect a "shadow" delegation to Congress before statehood was actually granted. The plan, which had been used successfully by Tennessee, Michigan, California, Oregon, Kansas and Iowa, involved electing a Congressional delegation without waiting for full statehood designation. Gruening and Egan were elected

U. S. Senators and Ralph J. Rivers as Representative. Although they were not officially seated or recognized, they attended Congress that year and were politely received. Bob Bartlett continued in his role as Alaska's lone Delegate to Congress.

Adoption of the Alaska Statehood Act

The adoption of the constitution and shadow delegation were bold moves. Two other factors were notable. In 1957 a collection of oil companies began exploration of oil prospects on the northern Kenai Peninsula. Richfield Oil Company of California was the first to drill and struck oil with its well. The discovery, reported on July 15, 1957, was the first major commercial discovery in Alaska. While important to local residents and several more companies that found oil in the region, the timing of the discovery was critical. Alaska, it seemed, had the economic potential for statehood.

Six months later, in early 1958, Edna Ferber wrote her novel *"Ice Palace,"* a story of conflict between fishermen and cannery owners in territorial Alaska. Ferber had already written many popular novels and had won a Pulitzer Prize, but *"Ice Palace"* presented a heroic story about Alaska's quest for statehood. She visited the state five times and collaborated with Ernest Gruening in her not so subtle advocacy for Alaska's admission as the 49th state. A reviewer for the *Chicago Sunday Tribune* called it "practically a love letter in fiction form to Alaska," the *"Uncle Tom's Cabin*" of Alaska statehood." Ferber's timing was well planned and generated substantial interest in Alaska throughout the country. Bob Atwood acknowledged in the *Anchorage Daily Times* that "Miss Ferber has rendered a great service to Alaska through her newest novel," adding that the book "contains a tremendous boost for the good qualities of Alaskans and their plea for self-government as a full-fledged member of the union of states."

Working together with Delegate Bob Bartlett, the Tennessee Plan delegation lobbied the Senate and the House. Influential House Speaker Sam Rayburn of Texas, a foe of statehood, changed his mind in the summer of 1957 and promised to give the territory a chance to be heard. When asked about his change in view, he explained "I can tell you in two words, 'Bob Bartlett'." Bartlett's patient advocacy, it seemed, finally changed the course of deliberations. With sectional conflicts breaking down and the power of the "Dixiecrats" diminishing, President Eisenhower stepped forward and endorsed Alaska statehood.

Representative Thomas Pelly of Washington State objected, demanding that his constituents have the same right to fish Alaska waters as Alaskans. He then proposed retention of federal jurisdiction over Alaska's fish and game resources. In response Eisenhower's Secretary of the Interior, Fred Seaton, explained the recently adopted model constitution addressed fisheries conservation and harvest issues. The *Fairbanks Daily News–Miner* responded by printing excerpts from Ferber's novel. The passages featured the character of Thor Storm, the grizzled Nordic pioneer, who told his granddaughter, Christine, about the legacy of Seattle and San Francisco cannery operators exploiting Alaska's fisheries. Ferber's book was well known and Pelly's objections were rejected.

C.W. Snedden, publisher of the *Fairbanks Daily News–Miner*, was a friend of Seaton's and recommended he hire Ted Stevens, a young Interior Department attorney who had lived in Fairbanks. Seaton quickly named Stevens his assistant for Alaska issues, where he helped draft and advocate the Alaska Statehood Act. With the help of Rayburn, Stevens and Seaton,

President Dwight D. Eisenhower, signing the Alaska Statehood legislation (seated center) with Vice-president Richard M. Nixon (seated left) and the Alaska delegation behind. Alaska delegation includes (among others) left to right Ralph Rivers, Ernest Gruening, Bob Bartlett, Territorial Governors Waino Hendrickson and Mike Stepovich, and publisher Bob Atwood. Ernest H. Gruening Papers, UAF-1976-21-289, Archives, University of Alaska Fairbanks.

Congress adopted the bill six months later. House approval came on May 28, 1958 by a 210-166 vote. One legislator said that the friendship many House members had with Bartlett was the reason for passage, but he still regarded the vote as "a miracle." The Senate adopted the House bill on June 30, 1958 by a vote of 64-20. Bob Atwood's *Anchorage Times* heralded the Senate's decision with the shortest banner headline in its history. In six and one-half letters across the page, the newspaper proclaimed in an extra edition "WE'RE IN." Sirens blared in towns across the territory and a giant bonfire was lit in an Anchorage park. A temporary star was added to a huge 48-star flag on the Anchorage federal building.

"We're in." The caption reads: " WASHINGTON, July 1--THE HEADLINE TELLS THE STORY--Gov. Mike Stepovich of Alaska holds a newspaper bearing a big headline as he stands between President Eisenhower and Secretary of the Interior Fred Seaton in the President's White House office today. Special editions of Alaskan papers carrying news of congressional passage of the Alaskan statehood bill were flown here by jet bomber for distribution to Washington officials. 1958". Candace Waugaman Collection, UAF-2006-154-8, Archives, University of Alaska Fairbanks.

Atwood's special edition was flown overnight to Washington. Enjoying the headline, President Eisenhower signed the bill a week later. A ratification vote, which approved statehood by five to one, attracted the largest turnout

The first Alaska Congressional delegation. Senator Bob Bartlett points to an arrow on a map of Alaska and the USSR following Statehood; United States Senator Ernest Gruening is on the left and Representative Ralph Rivers on the right. Alaska State Library, Portrait Collection, P01-3269.

in the history of the territory. On January 3, 1959, Alaska became the 49th state. In the U.S. Capitol building in Washington, D. C., statues of two outstanding citizens from each state are displayed. The hallway is a collection of famous Americans: presidents, vice presidents, framers of the Constitution and other distinguished Americans. The two Alaskans are Bob Bartlett and Ernest Gruening who dedicated most of their adult lives to Alaska statehood.

The New State of Alaska

Scheduled to become a U.S. Senator when Alaska entered the Union, Bill Egan ran for governor instead and served as Alaska's first governor. John Rader was the first Senate President and Thomas Stewart was Speaker of the House. Buell Nesbett was appointed the first chief justice of the Alaska Supreme Court. Egan had the most crucial role as the state's first chief executive. He appointed administrators and supervised the transition of Alaska's territorial bureaucracy into a state government.

Governor William Egan presents Benny Benson a framed Alaska State Flag design that was designed by Benson, ca. 1959. William A. Egan Papers, UAF-1985-120-7, Archives, University of Alaska Fairbanks.

As chief executive he oversaw selection of the state land entitlement, 104 million acres, as well as the surrounding navigable waters, perhaps 25% of all lands and submerged lands within Alaska's boundary. The new Alaska Department of Natural Resources held its first oil and gas lease sale in 1960 and oil companies rushed to purchase blocks in Cook Inlet waters. Two years later the Middle Ground Shoal Oil Field was discovered off Port Nikiski at the same latitude as the onshore Swanson River Field. By that time the state had already made land selections on Alaska's North Slope. With the discovery of North America's largest known oil deposit at Prudhoe Bay, royalties and taxes from these oil provinces more than realized the purposes of the state land entitlement.

Egan's other major venture was the fledgling state ferry system. Residents of Southeast Alaska clamored in the years after statehood for improvements to the antiquated federal ferry system, but the new state was financially strapped and some Alaskans did not want to commit financial resources to just 25% of the population. In 1960 the Legislature developed a list of capital projects for the first statewide bond vote. In addition to roads, schools, bush airports, hospitals and state buildings, the legislature proposed an $18 million bond to create a state ferry system.

Governor Egan was an ardent supporter of the bond issue, particularly expanding the ferry system, arguing new ferries would not only connect Southeast communities but also spur tourism. Bob Atwood disagreed, writing three separate editorials against the ferry bond proposal in the weeks before the election. The *Fairbanks News-Miner* agreed, but the *Anchorage Daily News* and *Juneau Empire* supported the bonds. They were approved by a slim margin.

Anchorage after statehood, All-America City, Fourth Avenue at night, February 1964. RG 77, Box 1, Folder 18, Construction Project Photographs 1950-85, Records of the Office of the Chief of Engineers, U. S. Army Corps of Engineers, Alaska District (Anchorage). National Archives and Records Administration—Pacific Alaska Region (Anchorage), ARC ID 5150368.

The first ferry funded by the bonds, the *Malaspina*, was constructed in Seattle and delivered to Juneau in January 1963, in time for Egan's second inauguration. The Alaska Marine Highway System has expanded ever since. Today it extends 3,500 miles from Bellingham, Washington to Unalaska, with 32 terminals throughout Alaska, British Columbia, and Washington. While most routes feature destinations in Southeast Alaska, others connect Bellingham, Southcentral and South-

Alaska Airlines DC4 in Nome after time of state-hood. UAA-hmc-0917-795, Donald A. Post, photographer. Donald Arthur Post slides, Consortium Library, University of Alaska Anchorage.

west ports. The refurbished *Malaspina* still operates today in a fleet of a dozen other ships, all named after Alaska glaciers. Four ferries are now retired.

In addition to administering the new government, Governor Egan encouraged investment in Alaska, noting its growing fisheries, oil and tourism industries. He also oversaw the state's response to the 1964 Earthquake in Southcentral Alaska. After serving the two-term limit set by the state constitution, he stepped down, only to be reelected in 1970, serving until 1974. During this time he worked to finalize Alaska Native claims and capitalize on the Prudhoe Bay oil discovery, two crucial endeavors that match his accomplishments during his first term. President Nixon signed the Alaska Native Claims Settlement Act in 1971 and the Trans-Alaska Pipeline Authorization Act in 1973. Both laws initiated important economic changes that heavily affected the state in later years.

Chapter Nine
Alaska's Geography, Weather and Extremes

*A*laska is bigger than most countries. It enjoys the most extreme weather, distances, and geological occurrences in the Nation, yet its residents experience volcanoes, earthquakes, floods and even global climate change as part of everyday life in the Far North.

Alaska's Geography and Weather

Alaska, the largest state in the United States, is 571,950 square miles (663,267 square miles when adding inland waters). It is more than twice the size of Texas and more than three times the size of California. If the state's western most point were superimposed on San Francisco, its easternmost point would reach Jacksonville, Florida, encompassing the entire Lower 48 states. It is larger than all but 18 nations in the world. With its many islands Alaska has nearly 34,000 miles of tidal shoreline, three times the shoreline of the remaining states. Permafrost and marshlands cover 188,320 square miles of the state, mostly in the northern, western and southwest flatlands, an area larger than California.

Because the Aleutian Islands extend into the Eastern Hemisphere, the state is both the western most and easternmost state in the United States. The original location of the International Date Line was modified in 1867 so the State of Alaska and all of the United States function on the same day. Once four time zones spanned the state, but in 1983 most of the state was merged into a single zone to improve communication and commerce. A second time zone exists in the western Aleutians.

Minnesota, Michigan and Wisconsin are all known for their lakes; Minnesota even boasts it is the home of 10,000 lakes. Alaska has 3.5 million lakes. Lake Iliamna, the largest in Alaska, is the eighth largest lake in the United States. Glacier ice and other permanently frozen water cover an additional 16,000 square miles of land and 1,200 square miles of tidal zone. The Bering Glacier complex near the southeastern border with the Yukon covers 2,250 square miles.

Alaska has the record for the lowest temperature recorded in the United States. It was −80°F at Prospect Creek Camp along the trans-Alaska pipeline on January 23, 1971. Barrow, located north of the Arctic Circle, has an annual average temperature of about 10°F and averages less than five inches of precipitation, so it is the coldest community and among the driest in the Nation. Even in July, the average low temperature in Barrow is barely above freezing at 34°F. The temperature in Fairbanks averages 26.7°F and Anchorage 36.2°F, both considerably lower than any similar-sized community in the Lower 48. In Fairbanks the average daily high temperature in January is -0.3°F. The Alaska Interior also sets records for the hottest weather in the state, with the highest temperature being 100°F in Fort Yukon on June 27, 1915.

The summer also brings longer daylight hours to Alaska, with areas as far south as Ketchikan receiving 18 hours of sunlight during the summer solstice, June 21. At the same time, daylight above the Arctic Circle increases to 24 hours per day. In Anchorage there are 24 hours of functional daylight during the summer solstice; in Barrow the sun does not set for 84 days. In contrast, winter brings shorter days and even perpetual night in the most northerly parts of the state. On the winter solstice, December 21, Anchorage has just five and one half hours of daylight.

The state has vast and variegated regions separated into five general areas:

1.   Southcentral Alaska. This is the southern coastal region that includes Anchorage, the Matanuska-Susitna Valley and Kenai Peninsula where the majority of the

state's population resides. The climate is mild by Alaskan standards because it is so close the coast. While it does not get nearly as much rain as other areas of the state, it does get more snow, particularly in Prince William Sound. The mountains that surround the Anchorage basin protect it from most of the moisture.

2.   <u>Southeast Alaska</u>.   This region is sometimes called the "Panhandle" or banana belt and includes the state capital, Juneau. It has large and extensive forests, the largest in the country, and tidewater glaciers. The climate is oceanic, meaning it is both the wettest and warmest part of Alaska with milder temperatures in the winter and high precipitation throughout the year. It is the only region in Alaska where the average daytime high temperature is above freezing during the winter months.

3.   <u>Southwest Alaska</u>. This is the coastal area bounded on the Pacific Ocean and the Bering Sea, including western Cook Inlet, Bristol Bay and its watersheds, the Alaska Peninsula and the Aleutian Islands. It is sparsely populated and not connected to any road system. It includes the Bristol Bay salmon fishery and serves offshore fisheries that are the most abundant in the country. The region is known for wet and stormy weather, tundra landscapes and large populations of salmon, brown bears, caribou, birds and marine mammals.

4.   <u>Alaska Interior</u>. This is the area of large braided rivers that traverse the state, including the Yukon and Kuskokwim drainages.   The Tanana and Chena rivers drain into the Yukon and surround Fairbanks, the largest community in the region. The Alaska Range,

The aurora borealis, commonly known as the northern lights, dances across the Arctic sky in this photo taken at Prudhoe Bay on a cold winter's night in 1969. Atlantic Richfield Company Collection, UAF-1982-146-10, Archives, University of Alaska Fairbanks.

with some of the largest mountains in the world, forms the Interior's southern boundary. The region enjoys the best views of *aurora borealis* (northern lights) and is infamous for frigid winter temperatures that frequently fall below 0°F.

5.   <u>Bush or Arctic Alaska</u>. This is the most remote and least populated area of the state, encompassing nearly 400 Native villages and dozens of small communities. The largest populations are found in Nome, Barrow, Kotzebue and Bethel. In the winter the region is well known for extreme cold and wind, with little actual snowfall. The giant Prudhoe Bay oilfield is found in the middle of the North Slope of the Arctic.

Alaska and the Ring of Fire

Alaska is in the center of the Pacific Ring of Fire, the well-known horseshoe-shaped series of oceanic trenches, tectonic plates and volcanic mountain ranges that cause countless earthquakes and volcanic eruptions. This is momentous for Alaska because the Pacific Plate is continually being subducted beneath the trench that encompasses the Aleutian Islands and Alaska Peninsula. This has caused periodic cataclysmic events like the 1912 Katmai eruption and 1964 Great Alaska Earthquake. The deep Aleutian Trench has been measured at a depth of 25,000 feet. Nearly every day agencies measure earthquake activity in the Aleutian Trench and in nearby parts of Alaska, although local residents do not usually notice them.

The movement of the Pacific Plate extends from the Aleutians along Alaska's Southcentral and Southeast coastline to the Queen Charlotte Fault west of British Columbia. Geologists have identified this area to be part of Wrangellia. This geologic region that is actively undergoing continent building, forms an arc from Alaska to Oregon. Further south, a portion of the Pacific Plate and the much smaller Juan de Fuca Plate are being subducted beneath the North American Plate west of the states of Washington and Oregon. Recent notable events in this area include the explosion of Mt. St. Helens in 1980 and the Nisqually earthquake in Puget Sound during 2001.

Active volcanoes are also found in the Aleutian Volcanic Arc. Unimak Island is home to Mount Shishaldin, a smoldering volcano that rises to 10,000 feet. It is considered the most perfect volcanic cone on Earth, even more symmetrical than Japan's Mount Fuji. In 2009 Redoubt Volcano erupted, a notable event in Alaska's volcanic history. In the last century there have been dozens of eruptions of Mt. Spurr, Redoubt and Mt. St. Augustine, all in the area 100 miles southwest of Anchorage.

Each mountain has its own special history. At the time of Mt. Spurr's latest eruption in August 1992 substantial ash was deposited throughout Anchorage because of the prevailing winds. The intensity of drifting ash swiftly turned early evening sunlight into dark night. The grit was so dense that automatic streetlights turned on hours before sunset. Residents were told to shut off their vehicles and airplanes to protect their engines and to stay indoors to prevent respiratory illness. Ashfall was significant, even in Yakutat, 400 miles downwind, and the plume was still recognizable when it reached Juneau the following day.

The proximity of the volcanoes to aviation routes means that air travel is frequently halted during their eruptions. Volcanic ash can cause jet engines to fail, so after Mt. Spurr's blast in 1992 the Anchorage airport was closed twenty hours. The airport closed and transcontinental aircraft were diverted around the volcanic cloud when Redoubt Volcano erupted in 2009. Today scientists at the volcano observatory track the moods of volcanoes and issue daily reports of increased seismic activity to news agencies, aviators, and the general public. Even with such scientific capability, earthquakes and volcanic eruptions cannot be accurately predicted.

View of the eruption of the Katmai Volcano in 1913 with clouds billowing 200 feet above the active crater. Alaska State Library, Subject Collection, P01-3586.

119

Lava plug of Novarupta taken from the crater rim above it. UAA-hmc-0186-volume 4-4528, National Geographic Society Katmai Expeditions photographs, Archives and Special Collections, Consortium Library, University of Alaska Anchorage.

Eruptions of local volcanoes are notorious because of their proximity to the population center of the state. The 1912 eruption of Mount Katmai was much more cataclysmic, but further away from population centers. Mount Katmai is a large composite volcano on the Alaska Peninsula located within the Katmai National Park and Preserve. The 1912 eruption is considered to be the most spectacular Alaskan eruption in recorded history. It is also one of the two largest eruptions in the world during the twentieth century. The 60 hour long eruption took place at a vent called Novarupta, six miles west of Mount Katmai. The withdrawal of magma beneath Katmai resulted in the collapse of the summit area, forming the caldera and draining the magma to Novarupta. The ash flow traveled 12 miles northwest

Marking the erosion of ash. UAA-hmc-0186-volume 6-H360, National Geographic Society Katmai Expeditions photographs, Archives and Special Collections, Consortium Library, University of Alaska Anchorage.

covering an area of nearly 100 square miles in what was soon called the "Valley of Ten Thousand Smokes." The blast transfixed the world and immobilized Kodiak and surrounding cities. Light ash fall was reported as far away as Seattle and fine ash was suspended in the air for months and caused spectacular red sunsets in many parts of the world.

Clean-up beginning in Anchorage on Fourth Avenue following the Alaska Earthquake 3/31/64. Alaska Earthquake Archives Committee Records, UAF-1972-152-151, Archives, University of Alaska Fairbanks.

The Good Friday Earthquake

The 1964 Alaska earthquake, known to Alaskans as the Good Friday Earthquake, began at 5:36 P.M. AST on Friday, March 27. It was one of the most frightful natural events of modern time. Lasting nearly five minutes, ground fissures, collapsing buildings and tsunamis throughout Southcentral Alaska caused over 130 deaths. It was the second most powerful earthquake ever measured by seismologists at a magnitude of 9.2. By comparison, the San Francisco Earthquake of 1906 would have measured 7.9, an energy equivalent of less than 2% of the Alaska quake.

Damaged Turnagain area following the Alaska Earthquake 3/28/64. Several houses have tipped or fallen into the settled ground. Knik Arm is in the background. Alaska Earthquake Archives Committee Records, UAF-1972-152-205, Archives, University of Alaska Fairbanks.

Turnagain neighborhood with cars upended after 1964 Earthquake. U.S. Army Corps of Engineers Photo. UAA-hmc-0427-14, Kenneth J. Huseby photographs, Archives and Special Collections, Consortium Library, University of Alaska Anchorage.

Damage to Railroad by Earthquake, March 27, 1964. RG 95, Box 3 of 25, Historical Photographs 1906-94, Records of United States Forest Service, Region 10, Juneau. National Archives and Records Administration—Pacific Alaska Region (Anchorage), HS 040204.

Damage to Highway by Earthquake, March 27, 1964. RG 95, Box 3 of 25, Historical Photographs 1906-94, Records of United States Forest Service, Region 10, Juneau. National Archives and Records Administration—Pacific Alaska Region (Anchorage), HS 040204.

Fissures and openings in the ground caused major structural damage in several communities, particularly in Anchorage, where homes, businesses and considerable infrastructure were damaged or destroyed. Property damage was estimated at over $300 million, $3.0 billion in current terms. As far away as Kodiak, two hundred miles southwest, the land rose by 30 feet. The land near Girdwood and Portage dropped eight feet and 20 miles of the Seward Highway and adjacent rails sank below the high tide of Turnagain Arm. It took two years to raise and rebuild the highway, tracks and bridges to pre-Earthquake standards.

In Prince William Sound, near the epicenter, a 27 foot tsunami destroyed the village of Chenega, killing 23 of the 68 people who lived there. The only survivors were those able to run to high ground. Postquake tsunamis severely affected Valdez, Whittier, Seward, Kodiak and other communities in Alaska, as well as people and property all along the west coast to California. Although Valdez was not totally destroyed, the town relocated to higher ground four miles west of its original site.

Twelve people were killed by the tsunami when it reached Crescent City, California, 2,000 miles from the epicenter. The tsunamis were observed as far away as Hawaii and Japan. Over 10,000 aftershocks were recorded following the earthquake. In the first day alone, eleven major aftershocks were recorded with a magnitude greater than 6.0. Nine more occurred over the next three weeks. Finally, eighteen months after the quake, the aftershocks subsided.

Interior Floods and Fires; the 1967 Fairbanks Flood

The summer in Interior Alaska is a welcome respite from cold and dark winters, but there are many challenges: spring breakup, uncontrolled forest fires and flooding. The weather patterns during the winter usually predict the result. If there is unusually heavy snowfall, the snowpack melts on major rivers too quickly. The resulting river ice can block river flows, flooding low lying communities along the way.

Recently in Eagle, a community near the Alaska-Yukon border, ice on the Yukon River was 55 inches thick—more than 40 percent greater than normal. When spring arrived in mid-April rising temperatures melted the snowpack too quickly. In less than a week, residents went from wearing snowshoes to swatting mosquitoes. While the Chena River Lakes Flood Control Project protected Fairbanks, low-lying communities along the Yukon were not so fortunate. In Eagle, the high-flowing river flooded the town. Large chunks of ice were carried over the riverbank and smashed into stores and buildings, lifting them off their foundations.

Each summer as the threat of ice dams and floods ends, the Interior terrain dries out and wildfires erupt. Wildfires in Alaska burn hundreds of thousands of acres every year due the combination of dry weather, lightening strikes and flammable spruce forests. State, federal and Native land managers work together in a cooperative response. Although fire is recognized to be a part of the ecosystem, the managers respond aggressively to protect communities, structures and valuable natural resources. Nonetheless, fire protection is a huge business with millions of dollars spent each year.

In July 1967, a month after the celebration of Alaska's centennial, the Fairbanks Flood, the worst disaster in Fairbanks history, took place. The flood was not caused by traditional ice jams on the Yukon River and its tributaries, but by unprecedented rainfall that turned the Chena River into a torrent. Traditional flood control systems upstream of the community and even sand bag dikes in downtown Fairbanks were ineffective to stem the tide. By August 15, 1967 the low-lying areas in the community were saturated. As the water crested all emergency response was evacuated to the University of Alaska campus, which is built on high ground in the suburb of College. Between 7,000 and 8,000 evacuees crammed into dormitory rooms designed for 1,000 students. Four people died and the damage ran into the hundreds of millions of dollars.

1967 Fairbanks Flood, with a view of a flooded parking lot and floating debris. Several parked automobiles are submerged in deep water. The steeple of Immaculate Conception Church can be seen left of center, behind a utility pole. Bruce Haldeman Papers, UAF-1982-146-10, Archives, University of Alaska Fairbanks.

The federal and state governments responded with emergency assistance, including low-interest federal loans, and the following year Congress funded flood control improvements. The project allows the community to divert the Chena River into the Tanana River if the Chena rises above a certain level. In 1969, Fairbanks was one of 11 cities honored as an "All-America City" by the National League of Cities because of its successful recovery from the flood.

Alaska's Glaciers

North America's glaciers are located along the spine of the Rocky Mountains and the coastal waters of the United States and Canada, but particularly where these mountains and waters merge in Alaska. There are thousands of glaciers in Alaska, though only a few have been named. Prince William Sound and the adjacent Gulf of Alaska are the best places to observe glaciers. The Columbia Glacier in Prince William Sound was once among the most prominent, but it has retreated almost ten miles in the last 25 years. Because many glaciers are retreating, the near continuous shedding of marine glacial fronts, called "calving," makes observation especially memorable.

Apart from a few tidewater glaciers, virtually all Alaska's glaciers are retreating and becoming thinner, suggesting greater declines for the future. This rapid retreat represents half of the estimated mass loss of glaciers worldwide. When John Muir entered Glacier Bay a century ago, the bay was filled with glacial ice. Now the area is in full retreat. The Juneau Icefield Research Program has monitored the outlet glaciers of the Juneau Icefield. They have found that 18 glaciers have each retreated a mile in that time. The lone exception is Taku Glacier, which has advanced fifty feet each year since at least 1890. The Taku's glacial mass has declined in recent years, suggesting even this glacier might soon retreat.

In Denali National Park all glaciers are reported to be retreating an average of 100 feet each year. Although the Black Rapids, Muldrow, Susitna and Yanert glaciers have surged in the past, National Park Service scientists believe these glaciers are also retreating.

Portage Glacier is probably Alaska's best-known glacier. It is located adjacent to Turnagain Arm, 50 miles southeast of downtown Anchorage. Most long-term residents can remember viewing the glacier from the Portage Lake parking lot and even walking on ice to the glacier face in the winter. The view was so remarkable that the federal government constructed the Begich-Boggs visitor center to showcase the glacier across the lake in Chugach

National Forest. By the time the center was finished, it lost its appeal, as the glacier retreated from view. Today a boat ride across the lake is required to view the glacier, which has now withdrawn from the lake.

Global Warming

Alaska has experienced widespread, adverse impacts from climate change. While the earth has warmed about 1°F in the last fifty years, scientists claim Alaska has warmed 4°F in the same time period. It appears that the state is in the vanguard of global warming, showing recent and pervasive damage to aquatic systems and wetlands, vegetation, ice, glaciers, permafrost, animals, and even the health and economy of its citizens. There are ongoing and heated debates about whether such impacts are human caused and, more importantly, whether the world population is willing to take action to avert the crisis. But Alaska has a ringside seat in the ongoing drama.

The analysis of the effect of climate change in Alaska consumes the world's scientists. Trees, marshes, permafrost, shorelines and floodplains are all carefully measured with satellite images. The scientists have observed the world's largest outbreak of spruce bark beetles, the decline in yellow cedar, the increased spread of forest fires and substantial shoreline erosion. The Arctic Ice Cap is a key ecological marker of Alaska's future, as scientists believe that polar regions warm the fastest. Vast regions of snow and ice that reflect 70% of the sun's energy to space have kept the Arctic Ice Cap frigid. But since 1979 sea ice has decreased by about 9% per decade, making it the smallest ice cap it has ever been, suggesting there will be considerable future biological impacts.

Animal life is particularly susceptible to climate change. Polar bears rely on sea ice for feeding, mating and resting. Because of global warming, their habitat is greatly reduced, causing Alaska's Beaufort Sea polar bear population to decline from 2,500 to 1,500 in two decades. Worldwide populations of polar bears are now considered at risk, if not endangered. Similar conclusions exist for other sea mammals such as gray whales, walrus and fur seals. Salmon and groundfish populations in Alaska's waters have also shown marked losses. While most salmon populations seem to be in recovery, recent declines were associated with climatic factors. Salmon populations in the Yukon River continue to decline and it is likely the river's warming and associated disease caused by such warming may be the culprit. Populations of crab, pollock and other fish in the Bering Sea also show signs of stress. While some crab species have been affected for a significant period, recent declines in the pollock population appears widespread and has caused significant reductions in the authorized catch of America's most prolific commercial fish species.

The consequences of climate change are likely caused by a combination of natural processes. Today most scientists attribute the accelerating rate of global warming to man made greenhouse gas emissions. Alaskans in particular are witnessing accelerating environmental and climatic changes. A landmark 2001 report by the United Nations' Intergovernmental Panel on Climate Change forecast that the average global surface temperature will increase 2.5°F to 10°F above 1990 levels by 2100. Ten years of change in the Arctic region showcases what will happen in twenty-five years for the rest of the world. As the bellwether for the Nation, recent observations in Alaska suggest drastic changes for the world.

Portage Glacier, Chugach National Forest, ca. 1965. RG 95, Historical Photographs 1906-44, United States Forest Service, Region 10, Juneau. National Archives and Records Administration—Pacific Alaska Region (Anchorage), 04010605.

Chapter Ten
Oil: Alaska's Black Gold

*W*hen the state government used its 1959 land entitlement to choose lands near Prudhoe Bay the oil companies were indifferent. At first there were a series of dry holes before March 12, 1968, when Atlantic Richfield Company struck oil at a drill site known as Prudhoe Bay State #1. Oil production did not begin until June 20, 1977 when the nearly $10 billion trans-Alaska pipeline was completed. Since then the state's economy has been irrevocably linked to oil with substantial revenues for the producers and, by virtue of royalties and taxes, for the people of Alaska.

Early Oil Exploration

Although Russians may have observed seepages, the first oil claims in Alaska were not filed until the 1890s on the west shore of Cook Inlet. But in 1898 the explorers struck more seawater than oil. The first productive operation came at the turn of the century at Katalla on the Gulf of Alaska. While some oil was found, lack of technology and the remote location meant the production only supported a modest refinery for nearby Cordova. It lasted twenty years until destroyed by fire in 1933, but showed that oil production was possible in Alaska, even if costly.

Congress adopted the Mineral Leasing Act in the 1920s to stimulate leasing of federal lands throughout the Nation and 400 exploration permits were soon issued in Alaska. Discoveries in Texas and Oklahoma flooded the market and drove oil prices down, making exploration in

Alaska uneconomic. In the meantime Congress created several strategic oil reserves, including the 23 million-acre Petroleum Reserve No. 4, now called National Petroleum Reserve – Alaska. The decision was based on U.S. Geological Survey exploration that found prospects in the Arctic, but little was done to pursue Arctic oil exploration until the newly minted state government selected and leased lands between the petroleum reserve and the Arctic Wildlife Refuge in the early 1960s.

The demand for petroleum during World War II caused the Army and U.S. Geological Survey to redouble their efforts to find new oil. U.S. and Canadian Army engineers constructed an oil pipeline from Norman Wells on the Mackenzie River in Canada's Northwest Territories to Whitehorse, Yukon Territory, and Skagway. Although soon abandoned, the construction of the pipeline showed new capabilities in developing oil prospects in the Far North. After the war, the U.S. Geological Survey also drilled dozens of wells in the Arctic, but they only found natural gas near Barrow, which has since been piped to that community to support its needs.

Swanson River and Cook Inlet Oilfields

After the war oil companies turned their attention to federal properties on the Kenai Peninsula. Richfield Oil Company of California finally discovered the Swanson River oil field on July 15, 1957. It tested at 900 barrels a day, the first significant commercial discovery in Alaska. A host of companies followed to find more oil, a new oil rush reminiscent of the fur and gold rushes of the past, as Phillips, Marathon, Unocal, Shell, Sunray, Mobil, Chevron and Texaco signed leases in the area.

After statehood the Alaska Department of Natural Resources sold leases in state waters in Cook Inlet. In two years Unocal discovered the Middle Ground Shoal oil field off Port Nikiski, the same latitude as the onshore Swanson River field, with production beginning in 1967. Since then dozens of successful wells have been drilled in both upper Cook Inlet and the onshore Swanson River

Field, the largest Alaska deposit discovered outside the Arctic. Though not well known outside Alaska, this area has produced over 1.3 billion barrels of oil and 5 trillion cubic feet of natural gas. But the wells are now on the decline and the local communities that depend on the reserves are anxious to find a replacement.

The impact of the Cook Inlet development on the Kenai Peninsula and nearby Anchorage was important to show the economic viability of Alaska as a state. The north Kenai Peninsula had a population of just 500 people in 1957. After the Swanson River discovery the local economy soared. Today, the population of Kenai and Soldotna exceeds 15,000 and all of the Kenai Peninsula Borough, which also includes Seward and Homer, is nearly 50,000. Although the region also enjoys prosperity from recreational fisheries and tourism, the economy of the Kenai Peninsula depends on oil and gas production, so with the local fields on the decline the economic outlook is delicate.

Prudhoe Bay Oil Discovery

Tom Marshall, who to this day receives little recognition for his accomplishment, was the State's land selection officer after statehood. Today he reports he simply chose the best prospects between existing federal enclaves on the North Slope within the Lisburne formation, a stratified section of limestone and sand 9,000 feet below the surface, but he admits his superiors and Governor Egan were uncertain if the state should even select the land. Once selected, the industry acquired the leases without much fanfare, as they thought the better prospects were further south in the Brooks Range foothills.

Prudhoe Bay State No. 1, the discovery well for the giant Prudhoe Bay field, is enclosed in a metal building in this 1969 photograph. The discovery well, drilled in 1968 by ARCO/Exxon, signaled the start of development from Alaska's North Slope. Atlantic Richfield Company Collection, UAF-1982-146-3, Archives, University of Alaska Fairbanks.

By 1967 both British Petroleum and Richfield Oil, the discoverer of the Swanson River field, had drilled a number of dry holes and they were about to abandon the Arctic. Richfield's final exploration program began during the winter of 1967-68. On the day after Christmas the crew opened the drill pipe and natural gas burst into the air. When ignited from a two-inch pipe it flared 50 feet in a 30 mile per hour wind, a dramatic and unexpected find. A second well was started to see if there was more gas and oil in the formation. On March 12, 1968, Richfield confirmed the gigantic oilfield. The following year, a new lease sale reaped $900 million in revenues in a few hours as oil companies purchased the fringe areas around the discovered oilfield.

Trans-Alaska Pipeline

Initially Exxon sent a reinforced bow tanker, the Manhattan, to the Arctic Ocean through the ice-bound Northwest Passage to determine if the route could work to bring oil to the U.S. East Coast. This showed the only reliable means to deliver North Slope oil was to build a pipeline, either 1,500 miles across Alaska and Canada, connecting with Midwest pipelines, or 800 miles south across Alaska to a warm-water port near the Gulf of Alaska. The shorter route was selected and a terminal site found near Valdez. But difficult obstacles stood in the way of construction. The first was resolution of the pending aboriginal Native claims to the land that the pipeline would cross. Passage of the Alaska Native Claims Settlement Act in 1971 removed that obstacle by granting Alaska Natives $962.5 million and more than 44 million acres of land.

A second and more substantial obstacle lay with opposition from the environmental community to the construction of the pipeline to Valdez. Several groups filed suit to stop the project, charging that industry construction plans violated the new National Environmental Policy Act. They had valid concerns. In its zeal to support oil development, the state built the North Slope haul road in the winter of 1969, dubbed the "Hickel Highway" after the then-governor who devised the plan. Once spring thaw arrived the road destabilized and in many areas with permafrost became a muddy quagmire that can be seen to this day. With this misfortune a federal judge granted an injunction to stop pipeline construction.

Summer pipeline construction pipe-line activity in Thompson Pass north of Valdez as the project neared completion in 1976. Alaska State Library, Alyeska Pipeline Service Company Photograph Collection, P02-3a-03.

Pipeline workers complete the "tie in," the final weld, for the Thompson Pass section of the trans Alaska pipeline project. RG 49, Box 91 of 97, Trans-Alaska Pipeline Photographs 1969-82. Bureau of Land Management, Fairbanks Support Center, National Archives and Records Administration—Pacific Alaska Region (Anchorage), PC2-22446.

As the oil industry scrambled to produce a better plan, Congress debated whether there should be a pipeline at all. To further inflame the debate, President Nixon appointed Governor Hickel as Secretary of Interior. Since the Brooks Range and other areas to be traversed by the pipeline were among the last vast stretches of open land in the country, national environmental groups insisted the area be set aside as wilderness and preserved for future generations. The future of the project was very much in question until Congress overturned the court injunction. The House of Representatives voted first to approve construction. Then in a dramatic Senate vote on July 17, 1973 Vice-President Spiro Agnew broke a 49-49 tie to adopt the Alaska Pipeline Authorization Act.

Construction of the Alaska pipeline began in the spring of 1974 and was completed in three years so that

Workers complete the final weld on Monday, May 30, 1977 at a site near Pump Station No. 3 on Alaska's North Slope, Trans-Alaska pipeline project. RG 49, Box 91 of 97, Trans-Alaska Pipeline Photographs 1969-82. Bureau of Land Management, Fairbanks Support Center, National Archives and Records Administration—Pacific Alaska Region (Anchorage), PC2-22446.

"first oil" was delivered to Valdez in July 1977. Over 28,000 people worked on the project, which cost more than $8.1 billion, exceeding the industry's 1970 estimate of $900,000. The companies completed the project in record time but at great cost. Both Standard Oil of Ohio, responsible for construction of BP's share of the pipeline under an acquisition agreement, and Atlantic Richfield almost exhausted their financial resources before the project was finished.

A separate company was created by the oil company leaseholders to build and operate the pipeline, the Alyeska Pipeline Service Company. It entered an agreement with the unions to use only organized labor to build the project, promising to pay high wages and provide the best food, housing and other amenities. For three years the workers turned Fairbanks and Anchorage into gold rush boomtowns. Unemployment dropped to near zero in both cities as Alaskans left their usual city jobs to take advantage of the windfall and crime rates and even murders were commonplace.

Since then smaller adjacent fields have added to the production on the North Slope. Development of these fields would not have been possible without TAPS and, in some cases, production facilities at Prudhoe Bay. For three decades Alaska's North Slope has produced about 20% of the domestic oil used in the United States, including most petroleum used on the west coast of North America. The early estimate for the field was 9.6 billion recoverable barrels. Today, technology has increased the estimate to over 20 billion barrels.

The impact of oil development on the Alaska economy is difficult to calculate. Alaska Department of

Revenue economists have estimated the state has received nearly $50 billion in royalties and another $50 billion in severance and income taxes on North Slope oil production, a total of $100 billion in three decades. The state's personal income tax was repealed and Alaskans instead came to rely on oil revenues to fund government operations. This reliance caused a serious bind in the mid-1980s when oil prices crashed. Prices had fluctuated from $40/barrel to $27/barrel in the early 1980s, but in 1986 the price fell to $6/barrel. The impact on Alaska was devastating. State government officials quickly cut spending, but the deep budget cuts meant a widespread loss of jobs, reduced incomes, and loss of business and property values. More than two-thirds of the banks in the state failed and housing prices plummeted.

The ongoing international energy crisis finally corrected as Alaskans benefitted from the actions of the price-setting conspirators from oil producing nations, the Organization of Petroleum Exporting Countries (OPEC). By the early 1990s the state recovered from that drastic downturn but the experience reminded Alaskans of the important role oil plays in Alaska's economy. Although the delivery of oil from the Prudhoe Bay oilfield is now on the decline, the pipeline's flow still maintains sizeable revenues, which barring deteriorating international oil prices should continue for at least another decade. State economists have estimated total revenues from the North Slope now exceed $300 billion. After state and federal royalties and taxes, they estimate the producers have enjoyed profits of about $70 billion.

Arctic National Wildlife Refuge

The oil industry and the oil-friendly Alaska Congressional delegation spent decades attempting to enhance oil production by opening new prospects on federal lands in the Arctic. The greatest prize is east of Prudhoe Bay in the Arctic National Wildlife Refuge (ANWR), which was set aside by the Secretary of Interior in 1960. Nearly half of ANWR is designated wilderness and is considered the most significant undisturbed region in the Nation. It encompasses a broad diversity of Arctic habitat, including coastal lagoons, salt marshes and river deltas in the north, and rolling hills, small lakes and rugged 10,000 foot mountains of the Brooks Range in the south. While the refuge provides important habitat for migratory waterfowl, it is best known for the annual migrations of the Porcupine caribou herd, which uses an area the size of Wyoming in the Refuge and the adjacent Yukon and Northwest Territories for feeding and mating. The animals winter in the southern portion of their range, where they are an important subsistence resource for the Native Gwich'in people, and migrate each spring to their traditional calving grounds on the Arctic coastal plain.

The expansion of the refuge in 1980 designated 1.5 million acres of the coastal plain as the "1002 area," requiring studies for potential oil development. Congressional authorization, long championed by Senator Ted Stevens, was required before any leasing could proceed. The debate inevitably leads to a comparison of the amount of economically recoverable oil and the potential harm of oil drilling on the refuge's wildlife, particularly the calving ground of the Porcupine caribou herd. In November 1986 the refuge managers recommended all of the coastal plain be opened for development. They also proposed to trade certain mineral rights in the refuge for a larger area of surface rights owned by several Alaska Native corporations, including the coastal village of Kaktovik. Conservationists were opposed, arguing that oil development would not only threaten the caribou by splitting their traditional wintering habitat from calving areas but also erode the fragile ecological systems that support wildlife on the tundra of the Arctic coastal plain.

In March 1989 Senator Stevens' bill to permit drilling was on its way to adoption when the *Exxon Valdez* oil spill occurred, delaying and ultimately derailing the process. But skeptical Alaskans consider the intense response to the oil spill as the reason for the state's recovery from the economic malaise of the 1980s, an ironic twist of fate.

Exxon Valdez Oil Spill

The *Exxon Valdez* had been in service just two years when it ran aground on Bligh Reef outside Valdez Arm in Prince William Sound on March 24, 1989. Equipped to transport about 1.5 million barrels of oil, the tanker probably spilled half its contents in the days following the catastrophe. The resulting oil spill was one of the most devastating human-caused environmental disasters in modern times. It was the largest spill in U.S. waters until the 2010 BP Deepwater Horizon disaster, but it ranks well down the list of the world's largest tanker spills. But Prince William Sound's fragile ecology and remote location intensified the consequences and, because they were slow to respond, exposed the industry's inadequate plans to protect the Sound.

After the Prince William Sound oil spill, a Coast Guard patrol boat from Station Juneau darts across the bow of the *Exxon Valdez* as the tanker is towed to Naked Island for temporary repairs on April 5, 1989. Alaska State Library, U.S.C.G. Activities, 17th Div. Photograph Collection, P313-08-18.

Although the inebriated captain of the vessel, Joe Hazelwood, is often blamed for the grounding, he left steerage to an inexperienced third mate, who was exhausted and inattentive due to fatigue. Exxon also failed to repair its sonar system so the third mate did not know of the impending collision with the submerged reef. At first Exxon used chemical dispersants to mollify the effects of the spill, but they proved ineffective. Booms and skimmers were then employed, but the skimmers were not readily available and the thick oil and kelp clogged the equipment. Finally, 11,000 Alaskans were hired to spray high-pressure hot water to remove the oil from the beaches and cliffs. The clean up effort probably recovered just 10% of the spilled oil; the rest was dispersed over 1,300 miles of coastline. Thousands of animals died includ-

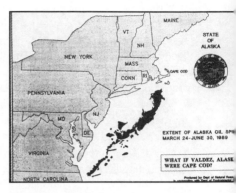

Exxon Valdez Oil Spill map, 1989, "What if Valdez, Alaska were Cape Cod?" RG 22, Box 7 of 189, *Exxon Valdez* Oil Spill Correspondence. U.S. Fish and Wildlife Service, Alaska Region (Anchorage). Records of the U.S. Fish and Wildlife Service, National Archives and Records Administration—Pacific Alaska Region (Anchorage), ARC Record 596645.

ing 100,000-250,000 seabirds, at least 2,800 sea otters, 300 seals and 250 eagles, and billions of salmon and herring eggs were destroyed.

Exxon was widely criticized for its slow response and was the subject of considerable derision and lawsuits from fishermen and municipalities most affected by the spill. In the large case an Anchorage jury awarded $287 million for compensatory and $5 billion for punitive damages, an amount then equal to a single year's profit for the company. But Exxon resisted the punitive damages award, litigating and appealing for twenty years. As Exxon's annual profits soared the litigation dragged on until many of the litigants went bankrupt or died. The punitive damage award was halved on appeal, and then in 2008 the U. S. Supreme Court decided the reduced award was excessive under maritime law, reducing the award again to $500 million. In addition to the resized 2008 award, it is estimated that Exxon spent $2 billion cleaning up the spill and a further $1 billion to settle related civil and criminal charges.

The *Exxon Valdez* disaster could not have come at a worse time for Alaskans who wanted to open ANWR to drilling. The legislation stalled for many years and public opinion prevented presidents Reagan and George H. W. Bush from taking action. In 1996 Senator Stevens and the Republican majorities in Congress authorized drilling in ANWR but President Bill Clinton vetoed the legislation. After George W. Bush was elected, Stevens again pushed for Congressional authorization, which was supported by President Bush because of the growing National energy crisis. In 2005 the Republican-controlled House of Representatives again approved drilling as part of the Energy Bill but, over Sen. Stevens' strenuous objections, the conference committee eliminated the provision. That same year the Republican-controlled Senate passed Arctic Refuge drilling as part of a federal budget resolution and as a part of the annual defense appropriation, but each time the language was removed. Stevens considered these repeated losses of the ANWR drilling legislation among his greatest disappointments during his four decades representing Alaska. Despite estimates of recoverable oil reserves that match Prudhoe Bay, the opening of the "1002 area" now seems unlikely.

The environmental community had unusual support in its struggle to protect ANWR. Long championed as a safe and benign to the environment, the aging pipelines at Prudhoe Bay gushed oil during 2006 from a corroded "dime sized" hole in the oilfield's gathering lines and more holes were found. Initial estimates said that up to 267,000 gallons were spilled over about two acres, the largest oil spills on the North Slope since the fields went into production in 1977. In November 2007 the feederline owner, BP Exploration Alaska, pled guilty to negligent discharge of oil, a misdemeanor under the federal Clean Water Act, and was fined $20 million. BP later discovered six miles of oil gathering line was corroded, leading to the shutdown of much of the gigantic oilfield and the loss of hundreds of millions of dollars in state royalties.

North Slope Natural Gas

Ever since oil was discovered at Prudhoe Bay there have been competing efforts to bring the natural gas associated with the oil to market. Talk of a large natural gas pipeline started during the 1973 OPEC oil embargo when several large companies, including most of the North Slope oil producers, announced plans to build a gas line from Prudhoe Bay across northern Yukon through the Mackenzie River Valley to Alberta. The cost was expected to exceed $20-30 billion. While considered the natural companion to the oil line at the time, skyrocketing cost estimates and opposition from Canadians demanding resolution of their aboriginal lands claims frustrated the project for decades. It also seemed each time the price for natural gas stabilized a new, more lucrative international find would materialize, making the project less competitive.

In more recent years the construction of a natural gas pipeline has become a political bellwether of Alaska politics with lines to Valdez or small feeder lines to Anchorage or Fairbanks gaining favor. Former Secretary of Interior Walter Hickel long championed some form of "all-Alaska" line so that Alaskans could reap the proceeds in another boom reminiscent of the construction of the Trans-Alaska oil pipeline. Today two large-scale natural gas projects compete for the interest of Alaskans. One is favored by some of the producers and follows the Alaska Highway through Canada to Alberta. The other, the Alaska Gasline Inducement Act, is supported by recent governors. Approved in 2008 by the Alaska Legislature, it provides state financial incentives to overcome the financial, governmental and land claims impediments to pipeline construction.

Presumably the ultimate decision will be based on the long-term market for natural gas delivered from the remote North Slope rather than the vagaries of Alaska politics. But time is short. Although proven reserves of 35 trillion cubic feet of natural gas exist on the North Slope, it is unclear if this reserve is sufficient to meet the minimum supply necessary for such an expensive project. Further, no new significant reserves have been identified since the discovery of the Point Thompson field by Exxon in the late 1970s. While there are significant remaining reserves of oil at Prudhoe Bay and in the adjacent fields, industry commentators have voiced concern that declining throughput of oil in TAPS may soon make operation of that line economically and technically impossible. Should oil production from the North Slope be shut in, not only would Alaska suffer the loss of its major source of revenue, but also the gas pipeline would likely become unfeasible for all time.

Chapter 11

Native Land Claims and the Native Community Today

*A*laska's thirteen regional Native corporations are now key participants in the state's economy, second only to the oil industry. Their rise to prominence reflects their considerable influence since the adoption of the Alaska Native Claims Settlement Act of 1971 (ANCSA). These corporations are among the state's largest employers through ownership of drilling, oil field service, engineering, environmental, service, construction, and other essential businesses throughout the state. They also own out-of-state businesses, some participating in the 8(a) government-contracting program, bringing millions of dollars of profits each year to Alaska, and dividends to their Native shareholders.

Impact of European Contact

The Alaska Native community has suffered many challenges since the time of first European contact in the eighteenth century. In addition to Russian enslavement and deadly battles, epidemic diseases reduced the pre-contact indigenous population by at least half. Smallpox had a particularly devastating impact, with well-documented coastal epidemics shrinking populations as early as the Spanish contact in the 1770s. By the mid-nineteenth century, the epidemics reached the four corners of the state, with drastic consequences for the Dena'ina Athabaskan population in the Cook Inlet region and the Yup'ik Eskimo people of western Alaska.

As non-Natives began to move to Alaska in increasing numbers, Native use of traditional hunting and fishing grounds diminished. Meanwhile they were often unable to enjoy the rights of white settlers, suffering segregation and racism similar to that faced by African-Americans in southern states. After World War I, businesses routinely posted "No Natives" signs prohibiting Natives from entering establishments; others, such as movie theaters, established separate "white" and "Native" sections.

William Paul and Elizabeth Peratrovich

In April 1925 the Territorial Legislature required that voters in territorial elections be able to read and write the English language. This literacy law was intended to restrict the participation of non-whites like similar restrictive legislation in the continental states. Yet there was considerable opposition even among whites. The opposition galvanized around William Paul, a Tlingit orator, attorney, and Native spokesman from the Southeast Alaska village of Tongass, and the Progressive Republican Judge James Wickersham, who both stood to oppose the literacy law. Paul joined the Alaska Native Brotherhood in 1920. This organization was a fraternal Native self-help organization founded at Sitka in 1912 to gain Native rights through assimilation. The premise was that Natives should abandon their language and customs, learn the English language, and attain their traditional lands through non-native means. But under Paul's leadership the Alaska Native Brotherhood urged protection of language and customs, agitating for equal Native rights and land conveyances of traditional lands.

Paul was the first Native to run for the territorial legislature, elected from Juneau in 1924. He quickly introduced legislation to blunt the impacts of the literacy law, protecting the franchise for everyone who voted previously, both whites and Natives. The result was a significant victory for Paul because his political base in the villages of Southeast Alaska was protected. However many illiterate Native residents throughout Alaska were still precluded from voting. Ultimately the fight required the support of white Alaskans, who were among the vanguard of Americans to support voting rights.

Elizabeth Peratrovich, a Tlingit born in Petersburg, joined Paul to advocate Native voting rights and prohibit discrimination. As Grand Camp President of the Alaska Native Sisterhood, Peratrovich provided crucial testimony leading to adoption of anti-discrimination legislation. Members of the Senate asked her whether an equal rights bill would eliminate discrimination in Alaska. She responded, "Have you eliminated larceny or murder by passing a law against it? No law will eliminate crimes, but at least you as legislators can assert to the world that you recognize the evil of the present situation and speak your intent to help us overcome discrimination."

Her response ushered the support necessary for adoption by the territorial legislature. Territorial Governor Gruening signed the Alaska Anti-Discrimination Bill on February 16, 1945. In 1988, the Alaska Legislature established February 16 as "the Annual Elizabeth Peratrovich Day" to commemorate the anniversary of the signing of the bill. Alaskans now remember her accomplishments, dedicating themselves to her efforts for equality and justice for all Alaskans of every race, creed and ethnic background.

Howard Rock and the Tundra Times

Advocacy for the interests of Alaska Natives jelled after Statehood when Howard Rock founded the *Tundra Times,* which was published from 1962-97. The paper was the voice of Natives and reported on the events that transformed their way of life, including settlement of land claims, founding of Native corporations, and transfer of health and social services to Native-operated non-profit corporations. More important, for the first time the *Tundra Times* coordinated the activities of the diverse Native community throughout the state.

Rock was an Iñupiat Eskimo from Point Hope and attended the University of Washington before returning to Alaska to get involved in the Alaska Native movement after Statehood. "Perhaps more than anyone else, (Rock) helped weld together the frontier state's 55,000 Natives for their successful years-long fight to win the largest aboriginal land claims settlement in American history," wrote Stan Patty of the Seattle Times. "He was their voice; at times about the only calm voice when crescendos of invective threatened to tear Alaska apart."

Rock had no journalistic experience yet a small newsletter intended to enhance communication among North Slope villages was quickly transformed into the source of information for Alaska Natives. The *Tundra Times* was nominated for a Pulitzer Prize in 1975. Rock was awarded an honorary doctorate from the University of Alaska Anchorage and was named "Alaskan of the Year" in 1974. He died at age 65 in 1976.

Alaska Native Claims Settlement Act

After adoption of the Alaska Anti-Discrimination Bill, pressure for more comprehensive recognition of aboriginal claims declined. The momentum finally came in 1968 after oil was discovered at Prudhoe Bay and it became clear an 800 mile pipeline was required to transport the oil. The ownership of much of the land along the route was claimed by Native people, so the state and federal governments joined with Native leadership to craft a statewide settlement of aboriginal land claims.

In the Fall of 1970, then Secretary of the Interior Walter Hickel met with prominent leaders in the Alaska Land Claims dispute in his Washington office. In addition to Hickel are (clockwise) Tim Wallis, President Fairbanks Native Association; Charles (Etok) Edwardson, Executive Director Arctic Slope Native Association; Eben Hopson, Barrow; Emil Notti; Attorney Barry Jackson (standing); State Senator William Hensley; Alfred Ketzler, Nenana; Barbara Trigg, Nome unknown; Delois Ketzler; Harvey Samuelson, Dillingham; George Miller, Kenai; unknown; State Senator Ray C. Christiansen (far right); Frank Degnan, Unalakleet; Moses Paukan; Morris Thompson; and John Borbridge (back to camera). Alaska State Library, Portrait Collection, P01-4686.

In 1966 the Alaska Federation of Natives (AFN) organized to address Alaska Native aboriginal land rights. In the following five years AFN worked to achieve passage of a land settlement to compensate Native people for the use of their lands. Once the settlement was achieved, it provided technical assistance to assure its implementation. AFN has also evolved to become the largest statewide Native organization with a comprehensive agenda addressing other issues affecting Alaska Natives. The annual AFN Convention is the largest annual representative gathering of any Native people in the United States.

ANCSA was signed into law by President Richard M. Nixon on December 18, 1971, the largest aboriginal land claims settlement in United States history. With ANSCA, the long-standing issues surrounding aboriginal land claims were achieved in Alaska without specifically recognizing tribes and establishing reservations, but instead by creating Native-owned corporations organized under Alaska corporate law. Primarily written by Senator Ted Stevens and a cadre of Native leaders, the legislation settled and extinguished Alaska Native aboriginal land claims by transferring $962.5 million in cash and more than 44 million acres of land to twelve Native regional corporations and over 200 local village corporations. A thirteenth regional corporation was later created for Alaska Natives who no longer resided in the state but it did not receive any federal lands.

All U. S. citizens of at least one-fourth Alaska Native ancestry in 1971 received 100 shares of stock in one of the 13 regional corporations. In order to avoid the premature sale of stock, the bill prohibited transfer for twenty years. These rules have since been amended to allow additional shares of stock to be issued to later-born Native residents and continue the restriction on stock sale. Most important, the corporations were required to share profits with their shareholders with minimum levels of annual dividends.

When ANCSA was first enacted, some Alaskans feared the corporations would either block development or hold it hostage, but this concern was quickly dismissed as the corporations undertook comprehensive profit-making purposes. Just as important, the ANCSA corporations did not simply develop their remote lands; they also helped reinforce the economies of the state's urban communities. Most of the prominent regional and village corporations have established corporate headquarters in major Anchorage skyscrapers, and Cook Inlet Region built one of the state's largest retail shopping centers at Tikahtnu Commons in Anchorage.

Over the years many projects were established on Native lands. For example, the Red Dog Mine, owned by NANA Regional Corporation, is one of the world's largest zinc mines and has been in production for decades on Native lands in Northwest Alaska. The Donlin Creek gold mine was discovered by geologists working for Calista Corporation and is on land owned by that regional corporation and a consortium of local villages. Arctic Slope Regional Corporation and Cook Inlet Region, Inc. are both petroleum producers that work diligently to encourage new exploration and production from their land on the North Slope and on the Kenai Peninsula. In Southeast Alaska, Sealaska Corporation and several village corporations are still active in the timber business.

While many Native corporations have enjoyed marked success, others have skirted failure and bankruptcy. Some of the challenges were addressed in the original legislation. For example, Section 7(i) was established to assure some equalization of the unequal resource potential of lands conveyed. It provides for the payment by each regional corporation of 70% of its mineral and timber resource revenue to the other regions. There were later amendments to ANCSA to approve land exchanges and the sale of "net operating losses." These tax benefits were purchased primarily by Wall Street corporations, which generated a combined $445 million in revenue for the Alaska companies.

By the time Alaska entered the 21st century, the major ANCSA corporations had total annual revenues exceeding $5 billion. Seven of the top ten Alaska-owned businesses were Native corporations. Revenues for the largest of these entities, Arctic Slope Regional Corporation, were

$1.0 billion annually. In a single year the Native corporations collectively distributed $117.5 million in shareholder dividends, employed 3,116 Native shareholders and 12,536 people overall within the state, and granted $5.4 million in scholarships to 3,040 Alaska Native students.

The Tsimshian People of Alaska

In the 1880s William Duncan, a Scottish lay priest of the Anglican Church established a Tsimshian community in British Columbia. After a dispute with the church, he was given federal land to move the community to Alaska, and he led 800 Tsimshians in a canoe voyage from "Old" Metlakatla to "New" Metlakatla in 1887. Later he secured reservation status for the community from Congress, which remains the only federally recognized Native reservation in Alaska.

Postcard view of Metlakatla, Alaska, ca. 1890. Box 275, Donated Materials in the National Archives, Henry S. Wellcome Collection, 1856-1936. National Archives and Records Administration—Pacific Alaska Region (Anchorage), ARC Record 297342.

Duncan's religious orientation was nondenominational, but quite evangelical. After resettling in Alaska, residents built a church, school, sawmill and cannery and constructed homes in an orderly grid pattern. Father Duncan continued to inspire and lead his followers until his death in 1918. The community is still located 15 miles south of Ketchikan on Annette Island. Despite the ravages of disease, it has maintained its unique character as a mostly-Native community of 1400 residents. The smaller Canadian community of Metlakatla is also still a thriving Tsimshian village of 100 people near Prince Rupert.

The Tsimshians were not included in ANCSA and although some residents are members of Sealaska Corporation they did not receive any specific payment for their land claims. They expressed an interest in preserving their villages and fishing sites on the Skeena and Nass Rivers as early as 1879, but have not yet concluded their land claims with the U.S. government.

Native Non-Profit and Tribal Activities

The accomplishments of the Native community are not limited to the profit-making ANCSA corporations. Because services to shareholders cannot always be measured by balance sheets, most of the corporations have established nonprofit arms. The largest are the affiliates of Cook Inlet Region, Inc., based in Anchorage and include Cook Inlet Tribal Council, Cook Inlet Housing Authority, Alaska Native Justice Center, Koahnic Broadcast Corporation, and Southcentral Foundation. Together these agencies provide a host of social, educational, medical and employment services to Alaska Natives, Native Americans and others living in the Cook Inlet region. Other regional corporations have established similar entities to administer culturally appropriate programs that assist individuals and families.

Tribal entities have been formed in many parts of Alaska in cooperation with the Bureau of Indian Affairs to facilitate the delivery of federal programs in rural Alaska communities and to address Native sovereignty concerns that were extinguished by ANCSA. But these tribal governments have a limited role. In *Alaska v. Native Village of Venetie Tribal Government* (1998), the U.S. Supreme Court ruled the tribes could not collect taxes for business transacted on Native corporation land or regulate non-Natives, because Alaska Native tribes (except for the Tsimshians in Metlakatla) do not occupy lands as traditional reservations, and thus they have no jurisdictional land base.

While there is considerable gaming activity conducted by Indian tribes throughout the Lower 48 states, tribal entities in Alaska do not participate. Gaming is regulated by tribal governments, Congress, the Interior Department, and the National Indian Gaming Commission, as well as by states under the terms of negotiated tribal-state gaming compacts. In Alaska, the unique implications of ANCSA and the lack of traditional reservations have thwarted efforts to formulate a tribal gaming authority in the state.

Formation of the North Slope Borough

Municipal and governmental activities are not normally associated with the Native community with the exception of the North Slope Borough based in the Iñupiat Eskimo community of Barrow, the northernmost community in Alaska. This governmental entity, founded in 1972, is the largest county-level political subdivision in the United States by area, a land area the size of Utah, 15% of Alaska's total. Iñupiat Eskimos have lived in the region for centuries, active in trading between Alaskan, Siberian and Canadian tribes along the Arctic coast.

The frequent proponent of borough formation was Eben Hopson, Executive Director of the Arctic Slope Native Association in the 1960s and one of the prime advocates for Native sovereignty. After enactment of ANCSA in 1971, Hopson rallied residents of the North Slope to form a governmental unit to provide community services funded by property taxes on the Prudhoe Bay oilfield. Several oil companies opposed the effort but the Alaska courts rebuffed them. In the decades since borough formation huge bonded debt has been issued to support the construction of extensive community infrastructure, including water, sewer, electric and other utilities, as well as health care and education facilities. Today the North Slope Borough is regularly involved in monitoring oil exploration, including scrutiny of offshore drilling in the Beaufort Sea and enforcement of the federal Endangered Species Act.

In addition to the Iñupiat, who dominate this borough's population, residents include whites, Filipinos and other diverse ethnic groups. More than three-fifths of the 7,500 borough residents live in Barrow, the region's commercial and transportation hub. Other borough communities are Point Hope, Wainwright Anaktuvuk Pass, Kaktovik, Point Lay and the oilfield base at Deadhorse/Prudhoe Bay. After the passage of ANCSA families from Barrow re-settled the abandoned villages of Atqasuk and Nuiqsut, which are also located within the borough.

Indian Health Services in Alaska

Today the Indian Health Service of the Department of Health and Human Services has responsibility for an array of Native health issues in Alaska. In Anchorage it operates the Alaska Native Medical Center, an acute and primary care health service that provides comprehensive medical services to Alaska Native and American Indian people living within the state. The Center includes a 150 bed hospital with a full-range of medical specialties and services. It also works in close partnership with rural health facilities throughout the state to support a broad range of health care services.

The Center has established a joint operating board with the Alaska Native Tribal Health Consortium and Southcentral Foundation to ensure unified operation of health services provided by the Medical Center. In addition to services available in Anchorage, the Indian Health Service provides health services in Barrow, Bethel, Dillingham, Kotzebue, Nome and Sitka. There are 37 tribal health centers, 166 tribal community health aide clinics and five residential substance abuse treatment centers.

Subsistence

Despite the long list of services and the comprehensive relationship with the federal government, Alaska Natives are legally considered distinct peoples, similar to the status of the Inuit and First Nations people of Canada. This means Alaska Natives are treated separately in some respects from other Native people in the United States. For example, Alaska Natives are allowed to harvest protected bowhead whales and other marine mammals under the Marine Mammal Protection Act of 1972. In addition,

Eskimo berry pickers. Courtesy of the Library of Congress Prints and Photographs Division, LC-DIG-ppm-sc-02306.

Alaska Natives were not included in the original federal Indian Allotment Act (essentially an Indian "homestead act"), but they were granted restricted land titles under the Alaska Native Allotment Act until it was repealed by ANCSA in 1971.

Yukon River Salmon, ca. 1913-39. A woman holds a king salmon while four men and boys pose with a cart full of large king salmon. A dog hopes for an opportunity to hold a salmon too. Dr. Earnest A. Cook Photograph Collection, UAF-2003-109-19, Archives, University of Alaska Fairbanks.

Probably no single issue defines the uniqueness of Alaska Natives as much as their continued reliance on the harvest of subsistence fish and game resources in the ways of their ancestors. Every year tens of thousands of Alaska Natives harvest, process, distribute and consume millions of pounds of wild animals, fish and plants through an economy and way of life that has come to be termed "subsistence," an essential component of Native identity and culture. Most Alaskans, Native and non-Native alike, want customary and traditional subsistence activities to continue. Although minor subsistence protections existed prior to 1971, ANCSA ensured that both the state and the federal governments would eventually enact subsistence legislation. The first state law, enacted in 1978, gave priority to subsistence uses of wild, renewable resources over other consumptive uses (such as recreational hunting and commercial fishing) but it failed to define subsistence "users." When the Alaska National Interest Lands Conservation Act passed in 1980, it mandated a subsistence priority, but in addition it required an allocation preference for rural Alaskans *(local rural residents)* in times of scarcity.

This did not mean that urban residents did not need or could not obtain wild resources, but only that the needs of rural residents would be met first if there were shortages. The federal provisions were to be implemented by the state, but powerful non-Native interests successfully challenged the state's rules, which were declared unconstitutional by the Alaska Supreme Court in 1989. This left the state without an effective tool for identifying a rural preference and placed it out of compliance with the federal subsistence law. A dual management structure began after the decision with the federal government regulating subsistence on federal lands (60% of the state) and the state retaining fish and game management authority over state (30%) and private (10%) lands. Since 1990, three state governors, eight regular legislatures, three special legislative sessions and a host of task forces, mediators and other efforts have all failed to resolve the state-federal subsistence impasse.

A unique subsistence resource in Alaska is the harvest of bowhead whales. The Alaska Iñupiat living in the coastal villages in northern and western Alaska have been hunting the bowhead whale *(Balaena mysticetus)* for thousands of years. Subsistence whaling became controversial in recent decades because of concerns about commercial whaling and the approaching extinction of the species.

In August 1977, the Alaska Eskimo Whaling Commission (AEWC) was formed to represent the coastal whaling communities to convince the U. S. government to preserve the subsistence hunt of bowhead whales. The government convinced the International Whaling Commission (IWC) to support this harvest, promising oversight from the National Oceanic and Atmospheric Administration. Today the harvest is regulated by that agency and the AEWC, with support from the North Slope Borough Department of Wildlife Management.

The members of the AEWC are the registered Native whaling captains and their crewmembers are from the ten whaling communities: Gambell, Savoonga, Wales, Little Diomede, Kivalina, Point Hope, Wainwright, Barrow, Nuiqsuit and Kaktovik. The AEWC is responsible for educating the outside world about the importance of the bowhead whale to their way of life. The harvest totals about 50 whales each year from an estimated population of 10,500. Conservationists fear this hunt is not sustainable but the current numbers suggest the population is growing.

Western Arctic whaling involves the shore-based pursuit of bowhead whales during the spring migration in shore leads (open water passages) during spring break-up. Some communities also engage in fall whaling when migrating bowheads return to their winter grounds. Hunters in skin boats (umiaks) traditionally threw hand-held harpoons at surfacing whales and, if killed, the whales were towed to shore. Aluminum skiffs and shoulder harpoon guns are used today, but the methods are similar and the dangers are probably the same. At the ice edge the whale is butchered, with the skin and blubber (muktuk) removed prior to sectioning the carcass and removing large amounts of meat for shared consumption by the whole community. Additionally, baleen (long sheets of bendable food filters hanging from the upper jaw) and bones are used by Eskimo craftsmen as raw materials for tools, utensils and handicrafts.

Alaska Native Heritage Center

In 1999 the Alaska Native Heritage Center in Northeast Anchorage opened its doors to celebrate Native life and traditions. Established on Native-owned land, the Center has become a renowned museum and cultural center for tourists, non-Native Alaskans and other people to expand understanding of Alaska's first people. Using dance, music, exhibits, craft demonstrations, lectures and an array of village sites replicating Alaska's many cultural groups, the center and museum are designed to enhance self-esteem among Native people and to encourage cross-cultural exchanges among all people.

Chapter 12
Alaska's Fisheries

*A*laska and her people enjoy diverse and abundant fisheries, a resource that has been intertwined with life in the Far North for millennia. Alaska salmon is "king," well known throughout the world as a wild species that relies on the purity of ocean waters and coastal habitats. However, many other freshwater and groundfish species support commercial, recreational and subsistence uses by residents and visitors throughout the state.

Alaska Wild Salmon

The commercial, recreational and subsistence harvest of salmon is closely linked to Alaska's history from early human occupation to its transformation as the 49th state. Wild salmon have developed a complex life cycle and thrive as five separate species: king (chinook), silver (coho), red (sockeye), pink (humpback) and chum (dog). Each species has distinct physical characteristics, habitat needs and timetables for spawning and rearing. Over the past twenty years, Alaska has produced and harvested ten times as much salmon as California, Oregon and Washington combined. This is principally because salmon in Alaska are intensively managed for sustainability and their habitat is largely intact, and salmon originating in Alaska does not face the same damming, deforestation and development challenges as those on the West Coast. Despite the fluctuations in harvest levels, the relative abundance of Alaska salmon and its habitat reflects the success of the state's management practices.

Fishing vessels at the Petersburg small boat harbor looking west from end of pier along public float, Wrangell Narrows, Alaska, January 8, 1948. ARC Identifier 298795; Records of the Office of the Chief of Engineers, 1789-1999; Record Group 77 (RG 77); National Archives and Records Administration—Pacific Alaska Region (Seattle), Seattle, WA

Alaska has not always enjoyed healthy stocks of salmon. The commercial salmon catch grew rapidly with the expansion of canneries through the 1920s, which led to such low salmon stocks that President Eisenhower declared Alaska a federal disaster area in 1953. By the time of statehood in 1959, harvests totaled 25 million salmon, 20% of current levels. The decline was temporarily arrested after Alaska became a state when careful monitoring, conservation and catch measures were instituted. However, advanced fishing gear and a change in climatic conditions lead to even lower catches in the 1970s. A statewide vote in 1973 adopted the limited entry permit system. This system is a complex management program that still grants annual licenses to commercial salmon fishermen in the state. The "entry permits" are a use-privilege that can be modified by a commission without compensation to assure harvest levels are maintained. A high proportion of local residents, particularly Native Alaskans, were awarded the initial set of permits. However, since the permits are a property right that can be bought and sold, over time many have been sold to urban Alaskans and nonresidents.

Fish wheel (outlawed at statehood for commercial fishing on state land). Courtesy of the Library of Congress Prints and Photographs Division, LC-DIG-ppmsc-01630.

Alaska is one of the few states where the management and utilization of the state's natural resources is guaranteed by its constitution, which provides: "Fish, forests, wildlife, grasslands, and all other replenishable resources belonging to the State shall be utilized, developed, and maintained on the sustained yield principle, subject to preferences among beneficial uses." The Alaska Department of Fish and Game operates with a strong conservation mandate to manage salmon fisheries on this basis, assuring sustained populations of the resource throughout the state. The primary management goal is "fixed escapement," where fisheries biologists ensure that sufficient numbers of spawning salmon escape harvest and return to spawn in the rivers and streams. Biologists open and close fisheries on a daily basis to ensure that adequate spawning occurs. If there is a run failure, managers close fisheries to provide for predetermined escapement needs. When run strength is strong, managers adjust harvest regulations to utilize surpluses.

An appointed Alaska Board of Fisheries has the responsibility for allocating the overall salmon yield between commercial, recreational and subsistence users. Meetings can last weeks as users jockey for position in the volatile politics of salmon harvest and management. Nonetheless, the separation of conservation and allocation authority between the managers and the board is one of the strengths of the Alaskan fishery management system.

Annual yields of salmon can reach one billion pounds in commercial fisheries conducted from Ketchikan to Kotzebue, as well as deep into Alaska's Interior. Salmon are harvested using a variety of fishing gear and more Alaskans are employed in harvesting and processing salmon than in any other commercial fishery. Bristol Bay is the largest red (sockeye) salmon fishery in the world and the most valuable single salmon fishery in Alaska. Pink salmon, the most numerous species, can produce statewide harvests of over 100 million fish. They are typically found in Southeast Alaska, Prince William Sound, the Alaska Peninsula and Kodiak.

Wild and heart-healthy Alaska salmon are popular with consumers and endorsed by most medical and environmental organizations. By contrast, the Atlantic salmon species is a high density, pen-raised, and sometimes genetically modified salmon, that has been the source of considerable worldwide concern for its impacts on consumers and the environment.

Sport Fishing

While the largest share of the salmon harvests are in commercial fisheries, there is a sizeable recreational interest in salmon, halibut and other sport fish species. In the past two decades the economic significance of sport fishing in Alaska has increased considerably. This is reflected in the number of jobs, wages and total economic contribution to the Alaska economy. Nearly one-half million resident and nonresident licensed anglers fish 2.5 million days and spend millions of dollars each year on licenses and stamps, trip related expenditures, pre-purchased packages, equipment and even real estate used for fishing. This economic activity supports as many as 25,000 jobs in Alaska each year.

Sport fishing is a vital source of income to towns and cities throughout the state. Over 70% of Alaska sport fishing occurs in Southcentral Alaska, with the principal beneficiaries being the communities on or near the Kenai Peninsula, particularly Kenai, Soldotna, Seward, Homer, Valdez and Whittier, where annual tourism is closely linked to salmon and halibut fisheries. But sport fishing reaches all parts of the state, with the Southeast and the Interior regions reaping 20% and 7% of total angler spending respectively.

Pebble Mine

Pristine freshwater habitats are the principal reason Alaska maintains viable fisheries. These habitats are regularly challenged by mineral and other natural resource activities as the state and federal governments carefully consider permit terms to balance habitat protection and resource extraction. This conflict is no greater today than in Bristol Bay, where the state government recently proposed a 1,000 square mile gold and copper mining district at the headwaters of two rivers flowing into Bristol Bay. While any mine development in the region is far from certain, the lines are drawn between those who support and oppose this designation. Opponents believe the open pit method of mining will use cyanide and other toxic chemicals to process the ore and store massive stockpiles of tailings in a seismically active area. If the tailings are accidentally discharged even after the mine is closed, the drainage will have a considerable negative impact on the salmon and their habitat. Proponents believe these issues are overstated and that the permitting system will properly guide their use of the land.

One mining company has already discovered huge quantities of precious metals in the area. To recover these minerals the owner proposes the "Pebble Mine," an immense project that will cover over twenty square miles of land incorporating the open pit mine, tailings, mill and tailing containment ponds. The controversy is center stage today and will continue to consume Alaskans for decades as residents and agencies decide whether and to what extent such a broad scale mine can operate in the Bristol Bay drainage.

Groundfish Fisheries

The state government regulates the Alaska salmon fishery because it is conducted within three nautical miles of the shoreline. Up to 1977, foreign fishing controlled the groundfish fisheries off Alaska shores outside this near-shore area and because there was no federal regulation, overharvest seriously depleted many fishery resources. As late as the 1970s the federal government would famously apprehend foreign fishing vessels that came inside the 3 mile limit, haul the captain to Anchorage and exact a huge fine for his release. But such arrests only underscored the concern for Alaska's offshore fisheries, which were unmanaged and commonly overharvested.

Senator Stevens and farsighted fisheries managers convinced Congress to extend the Nation's fisheries management jurisdiction to 200 nautical miles from the coast when it passed the Fishery Conservation and Management Act of 1976. The law is known today as the Magnuson-Stevens Act, after Warren G. Magnuson, former U. S. Senator from Washington state, and Alaska's Ted Stevens. Since that time federal fisheries managers and governing councils have adopted commercial harvest rules and conservation measures in a nationwide reach of over four million square miles. This fisheries zone is the largest in the world, much of which is adjacent to Alaska. Today the United States is the fifth leading producer of fish after China, Peru, India and Indonesia, with nearly 5 percent of the world total.

The Magnuson-Stevens Act required the active management of fish and other species in this huge area under plans drawn up by eight different regional fishery management councils and reviewed and approved by the National Marine Fisheries Service (NMFS). At the same time the Act provided for the transition from foreign fishing in the management zone to domestic fisheries, fully "Americanizing" these fisheries by about 1990.

In Alaska the North Pacific Fisheries Management Council is in charge, holding numerous annual meetings to oversee the harvest of five million tons of fish annually, about half the fish caught in the Nation. NMFS assesses and predicts the status of fish stocks, ensures compliance with fisheries regulations, protects and enhances Alaska's marine habitat, and works to reduce wasteful fishing practices. Under the Marine Mammal Protection Act and the Endangered Species Act, NMFS undertakes recovery efforts for protected marine mammals (principally fur seals, whales and sea lions in Alaska) working with the Council to minimize impacts to continued harvests.

The large continental shelf off Alaska's coast and favorable ocean currents in the region provide a rich mix of nutrients that sustain large populations of Alaska pollock and other groundfish species. NMFS conducts periodic surveys to assess the abundance of the fish populations and determine the total annual catch that can be harvested on a sustainable basis. When uncertainty exists due to lack of data, fishery scientists and managers employ a precautionary approach. NMFS and the Council work together to agree on the size of the annual catch.

After the annual catch is set, the harvest is monitored through the North Pacific groundfish observer program, the most comprehensive fishery observer program in the Nation. All fish are weighed or estimated by third party observers when the fish are brought on board and the fisheries are closed when the allotted harvest level is reached. Federal rules also ensure that a minimal number of fish are discarded as "bycatch." Federal retention standards are 85% or better and for pollock catcher-processors the targeted species comprises over 99% of what is caught in the net. These bycatch and retention rates in Alaskan waters compare very favorably with an average rate of 25% for world fisheries. However, in recent years the fishery has caught large numbers of chinook salmon, requiring federal action.

While there are many groundfish fisheries in the Bering Sea and Aleutian Islands, the Alaskan pollock fishery is the largest single-species fishery in the world. A member of the cod family, pollock reach maturity at an early age and produce plentiful young, traits that help them withstand relatively intense fishing compared to species such as salmon. Products from pollock include fillets, surimi, and roe. Some processors also make fishmeal from inedible portions of the fish. In the past several years, catcher-processors have increased the amount of products produced from each pound of pollock by almost 50 percent.

The fishery uses midwater trawling gear designed to avoid impacts to the seafloor and protect delicate species on the ocean floor. Pollock vessels tow large cone-shaped nets to harvest large schools of fish that swim above the ocean floor. Federal regulations prohibit "bottom trawling" for pollock. Other species are harvested using bottom trawl gear. These nets move along the bottom and in areas of coral and other fragile seafloor communities, with considerable regulation to avoid damage to seafloor habitats.

The authorized catch and resulting harvest of pollock has been declining in recent years and the allowable catch levels are now at their lowest levels in twenty years.

This is attributed to a change in climatic conditions. If the trend toward warmer temperatures continues, there could be further reductions in pollock productivity and catch levels. Nonetheless, the Alaska pollock resource remains abundant and has been certified by an international team of independent scientists as sustainable and responsibly managed under the Marine Stewardship Council (MSC) program. This program partners with federal agencies and the fishing industry to promote sustainable fishing practices through the adoption of MSC certification by global seafood markets.

There is conflicting evidence about the role of the groundfish fisheries in the decline of the endangered Steller sea lion and Northern fur seal, both dependent on pollock. Because of the uncertainty of these impacts, federal fisheries managers have established broad restrictions on places within the Bering Sea and along the Aleutian Islands. Despite the broad range of rules and restrictions, harvests of Alaska pollock average an astounding 2.5 billion pounds annually, almost one-third of all U.S. seafood landings by weight.

One of the principal features of the Magnuson-Stevens Act was to authorize quota or "catch share" systems to allocate rights to harvest groundfish in the many commercial fisheries. The term "catch share" has been used worldwide to describe programs of individual, transferable quotas that are usually owned as property by fishermen. Catch shares that subdivide the annual catch allow different fishermen to have different limits based on their historic share of the catch.

Under the catch share approach, threatened fisheries became sustainable because catch limits are set low enough to provide for sustainable harvest. This approach also eliminates the "race to the fish" problem because fishermen are no longer restricted to short openings and can schedule their voyages as they choose. Boom and bust market cycles disappear because fishing can continue through entire seasons. Safety problems are reduced because there's no need to fish in hazardous conditions just because the fishery happens to be open. There are fewer "fishing wars"

as fishermen switch from maximizing the catch quickly to a healthier focus on productivity of the species and optimal use of capital and other resources. Pollock fishermen have also formed fish harvesting cooperatives to help resolve problems of overcapacity, promote conservation and enhance full utilization of fishery resources.

Crab Fisheries

The giant "King Crab" of the Bering Sea. Courtesy of the Library of Congress Prints and Photographs Division, LC-USW33-029101-C.

Another important and well-known Alaska fishery is the harvest of king crab, which is conducted during the winter months off the coast of Alaska and the Aleutian Islands. The commercial harvest is performed during a very short season and the catch is shipped worldwide. In 1980, at the peak of the king crab industry, Alaskan fisheries produced up to 200 million pounds of crab. However, by 1983, the total size of the catch had dropped steeply due to overfishing, warmer waters leading to reduced larval survival and increased fish predation.

In Alaska three species of king crab are caught commercially: red king crab (found in Bristol Bay, Norton Sound and near Kodiak), blue king crab (found in the Bering Sea) and golden king crab (harvested along the Aleutian Islands). The red king crab is the most prized of the three for its meat. Specific size requirements must be met; only certain types of king crab are legal at different times of the year and only males can be kept.

The crab fleet went through a period of low quota and low price years in the late 1990s and early 2000s, leading to implementation of a catch share program. Under the new "individual fishing quota" system established fishermen were given quotas based on prior harvest levels, which they could harvest at a more relaxed pace. This system was implemented to improve safety and reduce through consolidation of quotas the number of vessels fishing for crab, as well as increase the value of crab.

Alaska crab fishing has historically been very dangerous with a fatality rate among the fishermen ninety times the fatality rate of the average American worker. That rate has dropped considerably since the recent federal "rationalization" of the crab fisheries. After the 2005 season the Alaskan crab industry transitioned from a derby style season to a catch share or quota system. Under the old derby style, crews competed with each other to catch crab during a restrictive time window, a dangerous "race for crab." The rationalization process reduced the number of crew positions as the owners of many boats sold or leased their share of the quotas, leaving only the most efficient operations. The reduction in crab jobs caused significant turmoil in communities like Kodiak. The political controversy over the consolidation continues today.

Alaska Beauty, 13th Region crab boat used to fish in the North Pacific Ocean. UAA-hmc-0384-s3-f3-23, Billy Blackjack Johnson papers, Archives and Special Collections, Consortium Library, University of Alaska Anchorage.

King crab are harvested with a box-shaped trap or "pot" that is essentially a steel frame covered with nylon mesh, weighing 600-800 pounds each. Most harvesting vessels carried 150-300 pots, making the boats top-heavy and prone to capsizing in freezing or turbulent weather. Herring or cod are placed inside the pot as bait and dropped 2,000 feet to the seabed to attract crab to the bait inside. The location of the pot is marked on the surface by a buoy. After a scheduled time the line attached to the buoy is hauled to the vessel using a hydraulic crane system. The pot is then brought onboard the boat and the crew sorts the catch, throwing back crab that does not meet regulations.

A crab holding tank keeps the catch alive until the boat reaches shore. If a crab dies in the tank, it releases a toxin that can kill other crabs, so the crew must be vigilant in removing any dead crab so they do not ruin the catch. Deckhands are paid a percentage of the revenues after the owner's share is taken into account. This can be lucrative for seasoned crew, depending on the success of the boat. Rookies are typically paid a modest sum because they are unseasoned and have a high learning curve.

The remote and dangerous nature of the work popularized the *"Deadliest Catch"*, a television "reality" series on the Discovery Channel. The show features the personalities of captains and crew as they struggle with the dangers of crab fishing. These hearty fishermen spend days at a time in rough seas working long hours with little rest. The most dramatic scenes feature deckhands hauling crab pots that weigh well over a ton as the freezing ocean water tumbles into the boats, washing seawater backward and forward through the decks, threatening all deckhands. The captain appears oblivious to all this, shouting and steering from the wheelhouse.

Community Development Quota Program

As the many offshore fisheries became "rationalized" and "Americanized" in the late twentieth century, far-sighted leaders like Alaska's Ted Stevens realized that many poor communities within sight of the fishing grounds had little stake in the fisheries. In one of Stevens' most far-reaching and memorable actions, Congress established the Community Development Quota program in 1992. The program promotes fisheries related economic development in 65 coastal communities in western Alaska. The communities formed six regional organizations, referred to as CDQ groups, that now participate in the federal groundfish fisheries by using quota allocations to generate capital and local employment.

The principal program objective has been to participate in the Bering Sea and Aleutian Islands groundfish, halibut and crab fisheries. In so doing, the six groups have secured industry partnerships, made direct investments in fisheries, invested in community development activities and facilitated training and education for local residents. In the two decades since the program was established, the economies and quality of life in the 65 communities has been significantly improved. At last count, over 2,000 jobs with a payroll value exceeding $25 million had been created annually in western Alaska. With a resident population of 30,000, the CDQ program has reached nearly every resident and helped sustain and enhance the economies of these remote coastal communities.

Alaska SeaLife Center

Alaska's marine environment is home to an incredible bounty of marine life supporting world-class populations of fish, marine mammals and birds that symbolize wild Alaska. Coastal waters around Alaska offer excellent opportunities to see marine life including whales, dolphins, porpoise, seals, sea lions, fur seals, walrus, sea otters and more. One of the best ways to gain an appreciation of marine mammals and conservation science is to visit the Alaska SeaLife Center in Seward. In the decade the Center has been open it has developed an outstanding reputation for understanding and maintenance of Alaska's marine ecosystem through research, rehabilitation, conservation and public education.

The SeaLife Center features state-of-the-art marine and freshwater aquariums with 30 separate habitats, each with several species, as well as other informative exhibits. This is Alaska's only public aquarium and ocean wildlife rescue center with more than 175 species and 2,000 living creatures on view above and below the water line. Visitors to this "window on the sea" have close encounters with puffins, octopus, sea lions and other sea life while peeking over the shoulders of ocean scientists studying Alaska's rich seas and diverse sea life.

Chapter 13

Conservation and Parklands in Alaska

*A*laska is a virtual subcontinent with countless opportunities to explore and observe a remarkable range of wildlife and topography in various climates. Within this vast landscape the "Great Land" hosts 15 national parks, preserves, monuments and national historical parks. The parks are larger in size than most states and more numerous than in any other state. In addition, there are many designated wild and scenic rivers, national heritage areas, historic and natural landmarks, wildlife refuges, national forests and the largest state park system in America.

Together these represent a natural and cultural legacy without equal in the United States and perhaps the world. But this rich heritage of protected parklands did not come without controversy and considerable effort.

Early Conservationists

The first notions of landscape protection came from legendary naturalist John Muir, the father of the national parks movement. He loved to visit wild places to experience the wonders of nature. Like Yosemite in California, Alaska was one of Muir's favorite places, where he travelled seven times. In his first trip in 1879 he mapped Glacier Bay by dugout canoe with Tlingit Indian guides. In the process he co-founded the small town of Haines. On the trip he also developed his notable theories on glacial sculpting.

On each visit Muir navigated deep into the inspiring glacier-carved channels of Southeast Alaska. He investi-

Muir Glacier and floating ice, Glacier Bay National Park. Courtesy of the Library of Congress Prints and Photographs Division, LC-USZ62-136267.

gated Tracy and Endicott Arms, but his most majestic encounter was Glacier Bay, where the main glacier had just receded to open the inner channels to exploration. Its main tidewater glacier was later named after him. He studied and reported on the abundant resources of the region and his observations of the Tlingit Indians. While he did not advocate parkland designations, he wrote of the grandeur of Alaska and a century later his writings on Glacier Bay were the inspiration of both the conservation movement and the preservation of Alaska's wild heritage.

The first to advocate wilderness protection was Bob Marshall, a forester, writer and wilderness advocate, who mapped much of the central Brooks Range in the 1930s. Defining wilderness as a social and environmental ideal, Marshall helped organize the Wilderness Society and fund its early operations. He was head of recreation management for the U. S. Forest Service from 1937-39 and, although he spent much of his professional career in Lower 48 forests, he first came to Alaska in 1929, spending 15 months in a one-room cabin at Wiseman. He explored the headwaters of the North fork of the Koyukuk River and bestowed the name "Gates of the Arctic" on a pair of mountains. He also wrote *Arctic Village*, the bestselling book in 1935, about the remote Brooks Range, the people of the region and his interest in wilderness preservation. Marshall's posthumously published book, *Alaska Wilderness, Exploring the Central Brooks Range*, inspired the eventual establishment of the Gates of the Arctic National Park.

Adolph Murie was a naturalist, author and wildlife biologist who pioneered field research on wolves, bears and other mammals and birds in sub-Arctic Alaska. After studying coyote predation at Yellowstone, he was sent by the National Park Service to study wolf predation in

Mt. McKinley National Park. His influential work, *The Wolves of Mt. McKinley*, reported three years of field observations from 1939-1941 and confirmed the social nature of wolf packs. His efforts led to the termination of predator eradication programs in Yellowstone and Mt. McKinley, as well as the expansion of national park boundaries to incorporate natural habitats. Working in collaboration with his brother Olaus and Olaus' wife, Margaret (Mardy) Murie, they worked to promote the conservation of Alaska's wildlife and wild places. He also wrote numerous articles opposing predator control programs and excessive human intrusion in wilderness areas.

Olaus Murie was also a wildlife biologist who studied Arctic caribou migrations and helped to establish the Wilderness Society. In 1956 Mardy, Olaus, and a few others spent several weeks on an Arctic expedition collecting data, making a film and reveling in the awe-inspiring wildlife-rich area. Armed with their evidence they spent four years campaigning to protect the region, enlisting people like Supreme Court Justice William O. Douglas. Unable to convince Congress to adopt legislation, in 1960 President Eisenhower set aside eight million acres as the Arctic National Wildlife Range (now Refuge or ANWR), probably Eisenhower's most important environmental action.

Mardy Murie was the first female graduate of what is now the University of Alaska, Fairbanks, where she met and married Olaus in 1924. She wrote *Two in the Far North*, a memoir published in 1962 that chronicled their Alaska research expeditions. After Olaus died in 1963, she flourished as the "grandmother" of the National conservation movement until her death in 2003 at age 101. She was instrumental in advocating the passage of the Wilderness Act and laws protecting Alaska's federal parklands. She received the Presidential Medal of Freedom in 1998.

Preserving Alaska's Federal Parklands

In 1963 the Wilderness Society held its annual meeting at Camp Denali, a wilderness lodge just outside the boundary of Mt. McKinley National Park. The purpose was to raise awareness of Alaska conservation issues, calling on state and federal officials to preserve wilderness areas. There was little response. In 1964 the Wilderness Act was adopted by Congress to protect nine million acres of federal land, but none of it was in Alaska.

Realizing that Congressional action was the best way to protect Alaska lands, in early 1971 a number of national conservation groups formed the "Alaska Coalition." Its purpose was to lobby in Washington D.C. to include conservation withdrawals in the pending Alaska Native Claims Settlement Act. Led by Sen. Gaylord Nelson of Wisconsin, the resulting Section 17(d)(2) of ANCSA required that Congress set aside up to 80 million acres of Alaska land in new conservation units within seven years.

den Creek Glacier, S.R. Capps 1916

Hidden Creek Glacier, S. R. Capps 1916, Denali National Park and Preserve. Courtesy of National Park Service, Anchorage.

In 1972 Interior Secretary Rogers C. B. Morton announced the "d-2" *withdrawal of* twenty-two areas totaling 79,300,000 acres of federal land. Further state land selections were suspended until Native land selections and conservation designations were completed, angering many Alaskans. Congressman Nick Begich called it a "massive land grab." Attorney General Havelock called it a "sell out of the people of Alaska." The *Anchorage Times* said it was a "dirty deed." The state filed a suit challenging the federal withdrawals, beginning a decade-long drama between the proponents and opponents of the conservation of federal parklands in Alaska.

The Alaska lands issue was forgotten during the Watergate drama of 1973-74 but in 1977 Rep. Morris

Udall of Arizona introduced H. R. 39, a bill backed by the Alaska Coalition, calling for 115 million acres of Alaska parklands, much more acreage than required by Section 17(d)(2). Udall said this would protect the environmental "crown jewels of Alaska," a phrase that would be heard often in the "d-2" debate, Alaska's "most spectacular natural environments, recreation areas and wildlife habitats." Udall sought to establish 10 new national parks and expand three existing ones, 14 new wildlife refuges and 23 wild and scenic rivers. He also wanted to enlarge the two national forests in Alaska, already the Nation's largest, and double the size of the national wilderness system.

Although the proposed H. R. 39 received overwhelming support in the Lower 48 states, the response was mixed in Alaska. It proposed that Natives would have access to traditional resources within the conservation units, so the protection of subsistence activities gained the support of Alaska Natives. But most Alaskans feared the bill. The *Anchorage Times* complained about "locking up" the mineral resources of Alaska, making the riches of the national parks accessible only to "butterfly chasers" and backpackers. Alaska was "pioneering country," former Governor Hickel told a *New York Times* reporter; it didn't need "a no growth approach." The editor of a Fairbanks weekly paper complained, "We were supposed to be taken in as a state on an equal basis, but we're not going to be allowed to develop the way other states develop their resources."

Traditionally the U.S. Senate does not pass any bill affecting a single state when the state's senators object. So instead of taking up the House bill Senators Stevens and Gravel persuaded the Senate to mark up its own bill. Although a Democrat, Senator Gravel also opposed President Carter's efforts to adopt the bill.

The "d-2" land withdrawals were set to expire in late 1978 because Congress had not implemented Section 17(d)(2) in seven years. Faced with the impending loss of interim protection, President Carter's Interior Secretary, Cecil Andrus, withdrew nearly 100 million acres of Alaska land in late 1978 under the Federal Land Policy and Management Act of 1976. He designated 40 million acres as study areas, preventing mineral or other commercial activity. Two weeks later President Carter withdrew another 56 million acres under the 1906 Antiquities Act, creating 17 new national monuments. The total withdrawals were 154 million acres, the most sweeping public land withdrawal in U.S. history. These withdrawals lasted three years until Congress took final action.

"Shocked State Leaders Try to Fathom Effect of Freeze," the *Fairbanks Daily News-Miner* told its readers. "Leaders React Angrily to Andrus' Withdrawals," the *Anchorage Times* proclaimed. Republican Governor Jay Hammond said, "It appears Alaska's worst fears have been realized." Some of the land was closed to sport hunting, Hammond said, which was "absolutely unacceptable." Sen. Gravel said, "I think it is clear the administration has overstepped the bounds of law," and the state attorney general announced an immediate suit to overturn the executive actions. But Charles Clusen, executive director of the Alaska Coalition noted, "President Carter has now replaced Teddy Roosevelt as the greatest conservation president of all time."

Whether Alaskans recognized it or not, they felt the weight of a growing national consensus in favor of the protection of Alaska's federal land treasures. President Carter and Secretary Andrus were the targets of resentment in Alaska, but their actions soon persuaded Congress to produce an Alaska lands act. At the beginning of the next Congress, Rep. Udall again introduced H. R. 39. This version urged more land protection than the original one, without many of its compromises. Senator Stevens recognized that a compromise was necessary because, without a bill, Alaska's future would be left in uncertain limbo. After the Senate voted cloture to silence the filibustering Sen. Gravel, Stevens guided a compromise bill through the Senate in August 1980. It set aside 104 million acres of new reserves, 15 percent less than Udall's bill.

Mount Eielson and Thorofare River, Denali National Park, J.C. Reed, 1931

Mount Eielson and Thorofare River, J. C. Reed, 1931, Denali National Park and Preserve. Courtesy of National Park Service, Anchorage.

In the 1980 elections Jimmy Carter was defeated, electing Ronald Reagan president and sending a Republican majority to the Senate. When the new Congress took office in January, there would be fewer delegates in favor of a strong environmental bill. Accepting this reality, Rep. Udall asked the House to accept the Senate bill, which it did. On December 2, 1980, President Carter signed the Alaska National Interest Lands Conservation Act (ANILCA), which set aside 104 million acres of Alaska land in dozens of conservation units. It provided national park protection to ten new areas and made additions to three existing ones, with 56.4 million acres classified as wilderness. It added 1.3 million acres to the Tongass National Forest, designating 5.4 million of them wilderness.

Though the name of Mt. McKinley remained, the surrounding national park was expanded and renamed Denali National Park and Preserve. The Lake Clark and Katmai National Parks and the Aniakchak Caldera National Monument were formed near the Alaska Peninsula. Along the spine of the Brooks Range a host of parklands were created: the Gates of the Arctic and Kobuk Valley National Parks, Cape Krusenstern National Monument, Noatak National Preserve and the Selawick, Koyukuk, Nowitna and Innoko National Wildlife Refuges.

On the Canadian border the Act established the vast Wrangell-St. Elias National Park and Preserve and the Tetlin National Wildlife Refuge. When combined with the adjoining Canadian Kluane National Park, this area comprises the largest tract of protected natural landscape in the world. On the upper Yukon River ANILCA established the Yukon-Charley Rivers National Preserve, the Yukon Flats National Wildlife Refuge, and on U. S. Bureau of Land Management land the Steese National Conservation Area and the White Mountains National Recreation Area.

Conservationists in America were less than enthused about many of the compromises, as boundaries had been drawn around lands of economic potential and some of the expanded areas were called "National Preserves." This meant that sport hunting, snowmachines, motorboats, floatplanes and chain saws were allowed in some park areas. In the Tongass National Forest, where pulp mills operated in Ketchikan and Sitka, ANILCA provided a $40 million annual subsidy. This was to ensure that 4.5 million board feet of timber was cut annually, a 35% increase. No other forest region in the country was supported with such a mandate and the subsidy was soon cancelled and the affected mills were closed.

Abyss Lake and Brady Glacier, Glacier Bay National Park and Preserve. Courtesy of National Park Service, Anchorage.

Conservationists also recognized there would be painstaking work ahead but at least the bill provided permanent federal land preservation and wildlife protection in Alaska. Writing 15 years after enactment, President Carter ranked this achievement with his Camp David peace accords between Egypt and Israel. He said that it was "one of my proudest accomplishments as President," an action that most Americans (and even most Alaskans) now approve.

In the decades since adoption, resistance to ANILCA in Alaska has subsided. Today communities that adamantly opposed parkland designation are thankful. The new designations focused public attention on Alaska's scenic beauty and wildlife, greatly expanding cruise ship and independent tourism throughout the state. Indeed, Alaska has prospered economically since ANICLA, as visits to Alaska's national parks have quadrupled to two million people a year. And with its base of operations in Anchorage, the National Park Service is now seen as a more significant economic institution than most mineral developments.

The best evidence of the change is found in Seward, near Kenai Fjords National Park. Seward residents initially revolted against ANILCA. The *Seward Phoenix Log* editorialized in 1980, "Many if not most Alaskans do not believe their state has the sovereignty, or shares the rights, of the other states." Two decades later, Seward reversed course. "Seward has done well by ANILCA and Kenai Fjords," the local mayor explained. "I think it has made Seward a destination

Pedersen Glacier, Kenai Fjords National Park. Courtesy of National Park Service, Anchorage.

spot. People go to Seward because they want to see the glorious Kenai Fjords National Park. There is a recognition that Kenai Fjords is a great part of our social and economic wellbeing."

Subsistence

ANILCA guaranteed a rural residential preference for the subsistence harvest of fish and game on federal lands. Native Alaskans in particular, but also non-Natives, have used these resources for survival because there is very little cash income and few jobs in rural areas. Congress simply recognized that new conservation units would present a hardship to such people if they were denied priority access to their traditional food sources.

The Alaska Supreme Court found this rural preference conflicted with the state constitution, which declares that Alaska's natural resources belong equally to all citizens. In 1978 the Alaska legislature passed a law providing a subsistence preference for "customary and traditional uses . . . for direct personal or family consumption, and for customary trade, barter or sharing." It was this law that Congress had in mind when it enacted the rural subsistence provisions of ANILCA, giving the state the primary role in subsistence fish and game management. In order to bring the state subsistence law into compliance with ANILCA in 1986 the legislature amended the earlier law by enacting a blanket rural preference for persons residing in the area where the subsistence activity took place. The Alaska Supreme Court rejected that law as unconstitutional in 1989.

The legislature has been called into special session several times to devise a new state system meeting federal subsistence requirements, but with the state out of compliance, the federal government took over management of hunting on federal lands. Public opinion polls have shown that most Alaskans support a constitutional amendment to resolve the issue, but some legislators believe the state should not change its rules, so federal subsistence management continues.

Alaska's State Parks

After the State was established in 1959, Governor William A. Egan proposed few state parks despite the generous federal land selections and, when he did, they were administered as a part of the Division of Forestry within the Alaska Department of Natural Resources. Presumably the state was not inclined to establish state parks since federal parkland advocacy was so unpopular in Alaska. Initially the state park system simply acquired former federal campgrounds, principally small roadside parks in the Interior and on the Kenai Peninsula. In 1966 the Legislature established the Nancy Lake State Recreation Area in the Matanuska-Susitna Valley, comprising about 23,000 acres. The next year the Chena River Recreation Area, about 14,000 acres, was also established.

Despite frustrations with its federal counterparts, the Alaska Department of Natural Resources established a separate Alaska Division of Parks in 1970, now called the Division of Parks and Outdoor Recreation. That same year three of the crown jewels of the Alaska state park system were created by the Legislature: Kachemak Bay State Park near Homer, Chugach State Park in Anchorage, and Denali State Park in the northern Matanuska-Susitna Valley. Kachemak Bay State Park can be viewed across Kachemak Bay from Homer. It has since been doubled in size, but in 1970 it was established as Alaska's first state park for fishing, boating, kayaking, hiking, camping and mountain sports. Today it now includes a wilderness unit and totals about 400,000 acres of mountains, glaciers, forests and ocean.

Chugach State Park is known today as one of the top ten state parks in the Nation. It is not hard to find, as it begins in the foothills of the Chugach Mountains behind Anchorage. It is a half-million acres of accessible hiking, skiing, camping, wildlife viewing, snowmachining, rafting and climbing in Alaska, the third largest state park in America. Despite this urban setting, resident wildlife such as bears and moose frequently wander into town, sometimes leading to anxious moments.

Denali State Park was established as an integral part of the greater Denali parkland area and was expanded to its present size in 1976. Its western boundary is shared with its much larger neighbor, Denali National Park and Preserve. At 325,240 acres, it is half the size of Rhode Island, and provides visitors with a variety of recreational opportunities, including hiking, photography, roadside camping and observation of Denali.

Perhaps the most remarkable unit is Wood-Tikchik State Park, which was created in 1978 as Alaska's most remote state park. Named for two separate systems of interconnected clear water lakes, this park is characterized by its water-based ecosystems. Visitors are attracted by superb fishing and boating in the Tikchik Lakes and Wood River Lakes, which reach 15 to 45 miles in length. Bordered by the Nushagak lowlands on the east and the Wood River Mountains to the west, these lake systems span a variety of terrain and vegetative zones renowned for their diverse beauty. At 1.6 million acres it is the largest state park in the United States. Private lodges within and adjacent to the park offer unparalleled remote and bountiful sport fishing. It is 300 air miles west of Anchorage and is accessible by charter flight from Dillingham.

Alaska's state park system has been expanded many times to include both large and small parks as well as wilderness and roadside camping. There are historical and marine parks, glaciers and totem poles, and parks teeming with wildlife and nesting bald eagles. It is the largest and most varied of all the park systems in the Nation, dwarfing any of its competitors in size, beauty, diversity and vitality.

Alaska Conservation Today

The conservation movement in Alaska is more energetic than in any other place in the Nation. The tradition of Muir, Marshall and the Muries has matured with the adoption of ANILCA. Once unpopular among many residents and state leaders, conservationists are now expected to scrutinize proposed developments on federal, state and Native lands.

The first citizen conservation organization with statewide pretensions was the Alaska Conservation Society, founded in Fairbanks shortly after statehood by Celia Hunter and Ginny Wood. It cut its teeth in halting the ill-conceived Rampart Dam and nuclear Project Chariot proposals. Later other Alaska-based conservation groups grew beyond the all-volunteer stage, including the Alaska Center for the Environment in Anchorage, the Southeast Alaska Conservation Council in Juneau and the Northern Alaska Environmental Center in Fairbanks.

With the formation of the Alaska Coalition, national attention focused on Alaska and the need to support local conservation efforts. Former Sierra Club financial advisor Denny Wilcher joined with Alaska conservationists, led by Celia Hunter, to form the Alaska Conservation Foundation when ANILCA was adopted in 1980. It started small, raising less than half a million dollars a year but in two decades it brought in about $2 million a year to support Alaska conservation efforts, principally the three community-based organizations in Anchorage, Juneau and Fairbanks. As national attention has focused on Alaska, it continued to succeed, raising more than $7 million annually. Along the way, it has facilitated implementation of ANILCA, supported opposition to questionable projects, investigated the effects of global warming and nurtured a wide range of citizen conservation groups.

Chapter 14
Alaska Today

"North to the Future" is Alaska's motto, adopted in 1967 to celebrate the centennial of the Alaska Purchase and the optimism of Alaskans after statehood. The state has now celebrated its first half-century recovering from the cataclysmic 1964 earthquake and 1967 Fairbanks flood to establish the 49th state as an enduring symbol of the potential of the Far North.

In the decades since statehood, many leaders emerged, but five prominent residents offered their unique talents to shape the state's development and secure Alaska's prominence in the National conscience. While many people deserve recognition, Ted Stevens, Jay Hammond, Walter Hickel, Elmer Rasmuson and Sarah Palin are the most well-known and celebrated Alaskans who have inspired Americans in the modern era.

Ted Stevens

Ted Stevens is a household name in Alaska. He was named "Alaskan of the Century" by Alaskan of the Year Committee and was known as its biggest advocate and favorite uncle, representing Alaska in the U. S. Senate for four decades. He served as a pilot during World War II resupplying troops in China and was awarded the Distinguished Flying Cross. Arriving in Fairbanks after law school in the 1950s, he returned to the Nation's capital to assist the Secretary of the Interior on Alaska issues. He helped shape the Statehood Act, promoted its passage and in the process formed a life-long bond with public policy issues affecting the state.

Senator Ted Stevens, ca. 2010.
Courtesy of Stevens Family.

Stevens returned to Alaska after statehood and in 1964 he won a seat in the state legislature before being appointed by then-Governor Hickel to serve the remaining term of Senator Bob Bartlett, who died in office in 1968. Stevens was re-elected with little opposition many times to lead Alaskans through the challenges of a new and growing state. In the Senate, he served as President Pro Tempore, third in line to the Presidency, and chaired the powerful Senate Appropriations Committee. Known for his volatile temper and unrestrained advocacy for Alaska, he was the longest-serving Republican in the Senate's history.

Stevens was the architect of most legislation affecting Alaska, including the Statehood Act, Alaska Native Claims Settlement Act, Alaska National Interest Lands Conservation Act and Magnuson-Stevens Fishery Conservation and Management Act. He was instrumental in facilitating rural health and infrastructure, public broadcasting, aircraft safety, universal phone services, the 200 mile limit, community development and fishing quotas, women's sports, the modern Olympics and construction of the trans-Alaska oil pipeline. He was probably best known for his considerable public works and military appropriations, which endeared him to most Alaskans as their "Uncle Ted." He became an economic force that was second only to the oil industry. Perhaps his greatest disappointment was the inability to secure Congressional approval for drilling in the Arctic National Wildlife Refuge.

Stevens died at age 86 in a tragic airplane accident near a Bristol Bay fishing lodge on August 9, 2010. "He loved Alaska with all his heart," the family explained after his death. "He was a guiding light through statehood and the development of the 49th state. Now that light is gone but the warmth and radiance of his life and his work will shine forever in the last frontier. His legacy is the 49th star on the American Flag." After his death Congress named both a 13,895 foot peak in Denali National Park and a massive ice field between Anchorage and Valdez after the longtime senator.

Jay Hammond

Jay Hammond was Alaska's Governor from 1974 to 1982, when the trans-Alaska oil pipeline was constructed and Prudhoe Bay oil was first delivered that swelled the state's budget and economy. He preached fiscal conservatism to steer a significant part of the oil revenues into a state savings account while advocating moderation and state-federal cooperation during the federal parklands debate that enveloped the state.

Hammond came to Alaska after serving as a Marine fighter pilot during World War II. He bought an amphibious plane and worked as a bush pilot and trapper, earning a biology degree from the University of Alaska. He and his wife, Bella, homesteaded in a remote area near Lake Clark before statehood, where he developed a unique perspective about the Alaska environment, insisting that development not proceed at the expense of environmental protection. He was elected to the state legislature in 1959 and served several terms. He then became mayor of the Bristol Bay Borough and was elected a state senator.

Jay and Bella Hammond under lines of drying salmon fillets. Alaska State Library, Alaska Office of the Governor Photograph Collection, P213-4-035.

While he was Governor, he oversaw the building and opening of the trans-Alaska Pipeline. He strongly advocated preservation of a large portion of the oil lease and royalty revenues in the Alaska Permanent Fund. He was concerned that the one-time revenues might be quickly dissipated, so urged Alaskans to save their oil income for the future.

He was governor when the National frenzy over parkland protection for Alaska's federal lands reached its zenith. Despite local hostility he led Alaskans with a measured response that recognized the importance of agency cooperation, environmental preservation and continued hunting and fishing in Alaska's rural communities.

Hammond was a humble man and displayed a warm sense of humor. During a re-election debate in 1978 he was asked if he believed he was the best choice to be Governor. Hammond replied, "No, there are plenty of other Alaskans who can do a much better job than I could. Unfortunately, none of them are running." He wrote *Tales of Alaska's Bush Rat Governor: The Extraordinary Autobiography of Jay Hammond, Wilderness Guide and Reluctant Politician*, published in 1996. He died on his Lake Clark homestead on August 2, 2005 at age 83.

Walter Hickel

Walter Hickel was twice Governor of Alaska, elected in 1966 as a Republican and in 1990 under the banner of the Alaska Independence Party. Arriving in Alaska in 1940, he successfully built shopping centers, subdivisions and the state's finest hotel, the Hotel Captain Cook. He was politically active by 1952 when he joined the statehood campaign, lobbying for Alaska to receive a land entitlement of at least 100 million acres. Public policy was important to Hickel all his life. After statehood he championed issues affecting Alaska's natural resources, helped open the North Slope to oil development, and worked on worldwide northern region issues.

Governor Walter and Ermalee Hickel in Homer, 1993. Courtesy of John Hendrickson and Malcolm Roberts.

In 1969 he became Secretary of the Interior under President Richard Nixon. As Secretary, he advocated for a national energy policy and environmental protection. His actions as Secretary were detailed in his book, *Who Owns America?* and included upgrading offshore oil drilling regulations after the 1969 Santa Barbara oil spill. He advocated for the Alaska Native Claims Settlement Act, placed eight species of whales on the Endangered Species List, and was responsible for a multitude of other precedent-setting actions on behalf of the Nation's public resources. He sent a letter to the President about the White House attitude towards America's young people who opposed the Vietnam War that was leaked to the press. In addition to his firm dealing with oil industry abuses of the environment, this letter led to his firing on November 25, 1970.

In June 1982 then-Governor Jay Hammond asked former Governors Hickel and Egan to lead an effort to explore alternatives to bring Alaska's North Slope natural gas to market. They proposed the construction of an 820 mile gas pipeline from Prudhoe Bay to Valdez to serve Alaska, the West Coast and Pacific Rim markets, the "All-Alaska" route he championed for the rest of his life. Named as the "Alaskan of the Year" in 1969, Hickel received 12 honorary college degrees and wrote several books, including *Crisis in the Commons: the Alaska Solution,* when he was 82. He died in 2010 at age 90 and is remembered as an Arctic statesman and visionary.

Elmer Rasmuson

Elmer E. Rasmuson was born in Yakutat to Swedish missionary immigrants. His father settled in Skagway, where he served as magistrate and later took over a struggling bank, the Bank of Alaska. He left Skagway for schooling but returned to take the presidency of the bank when his father became ill. He moved the bank's headquarters to Anchorage in 1945. He inherited a controlling interest in the bank when his father passed away in 1949. It became the National Bank of Alaska in 1950 when it adopted a national charter.

Capitalizing on profits from the Swanson River oil field and the bustling post-statehood economy, the National Bank of Alaska became the largest bank in the state, with 16 branches. Dismayed by what he considered a disorganized response to the 1964 Earthquake, Rasmuson ran for mayor of Anchorage and served until 1967, overseeing much of the reconstruction. In 1968 he ran in the Republican primary for the U.S. Senate and beat his competitor, Ted Stevens. But he lost in the general election to Democrat Mike Gravel. After Stevens was named to the open seat after Bob Bartlett's death, Rasmuson left politics. He retired from active management of the bank in 1975. As he had succeeded his father, Elmer's son, Edward B., succeeded him in managing the bank until it was sold to Wells Fargo & Co. in 1999.

As the bank prospered after statehood, Rasmuson used his money to support arts and education throughout the Alaska.

Elmer and Mary Louise Rasmuson. Courtesy of Rasmuson Foundation.

His most notable contributions were made to the University of Alaska, where he served as a regent from 1950-69, and museums in Anchorage and Fairbanks. He endowed a small family foundation with his considerable wealth and it quickly flourished, operating today as a significant resource for non-profit organizations throughout the state. "Having provided substantially for the members of my family, I decided some years ago that my entire estate would be channeled to charitable and public benefit," he told celebrants at his 90th birthday party.

Elmer passed the leadership of his charity to his second wife, Mary Louise, as well as his son Ed, who now serves as the Foundation chair. In recent years the Rasmuson Foundation has become the most generous private donor in Alaska, handing out millions of dollars of annual grants for arts, culture, social and community causes. It has become a powerful statewide force that has changed the face of Alaska's social conscience for the good. Elmer died in a Seattle hospital at age 91 on December 1, 2000.

Sarah Palin

Sarah Palin is perhaps the most well-known and controversial person from Alaska. She was elected Mayor of Wasilla and Governor of Alaska before exploding on the National stage when Senator John McCain selected her as his Vice Presidential running mate in August 2008. She was the first Alaskan on the national ticket of a major party and the first female vice-presidential nominee of the Republican Party. Though defeated in the election, she remained a stalwart of the conservative element of the party and is frequently mentioned as a potential presidential nominee.

Alaska Gov. Sarah Palin was the vice presidential running mate of 2008 Republican presidential candidate Sen. John McCain of Arizona. Photo by Al Grillo

Palin was born in Idaho and moved to Skagway, Alaska as an infant. She was point guard of the state champion women's high school basketball team and attended a number of colleges before graduating from the University of Idaho in 1986. After graduation she was an Anchorage sportscaster before eloping with her childhood sweetheart, Todd Palin of Dillingham. While their principal income came from Todd's work in the oil industry, they also operated a Bristol Bay set net site harvesting sockeye salmon each summer. They have five children.

Palin was a member of the Wasilla city council from 1992-96 and was mayor from 1996-2002. After an unsuccessful campaign for lieutenant governor in 2002, she was appointed by then-Governor Frank Murkowski to chair the Alaska Oil and Gas Conservation Commission. She resigned her seat after a dispute with a fellow commissioner, the chair of the Republican Party, who leaked a confidential commission document to the oil industry. Her irritation with ethical concerns vaulted her to prominence in Alaska, where she ran against the party leadership (including Governor Murkowski) and was elected Governor in 2006.

During most of her term as Governor she was very popular with Alaska voters. Some polls suggested she had a 93% favorable rating, perhaps the most popular politician in America. Her term as Governor was consumed with a bipartisan effort to license the construction of the Alaska natural gas pipeline to a Canadian firm. Soon after the license was approved, McCain tapped her to run as his Vice Presidential candidate. The call came when she was attending the Alaska State Fair. She was a vibrant and aggressive candidate, although the National media questioned her qualifications after unscripted encounters with the press.

She returned to the state following the presidential election and on July 3, 2009, Palin resigned as Governor, eighteen months before her term was finished. She cited the personal cost of defending herself against ethics complaints filed after her selection as McCain's running mate as part of the reason for her resignation. Despite the resignation, she remains one of America's most influential politicians, endorsing and campaigning for conservative Republicans with considerable success. In 2008 she was selected as one of America's "Top 10 Most Fascinating People" by Barbara Walters and one of the 100 World's Most Influential People by *TIME Magazine*.

Alaska's Future

Since the time of European occupation and the advent of a western economy, Alaska's history has depended on the boom and bust cycles of resource extraction. First the Russians and their competitors overwhelmed the local people in an obsession for fur, hunting the sea otter to virtual extinction. After the Americans took over, these cycles continued with a series of gold rushes in the late 19th century, followed by the exploitation of salmon, military expansion and oil development. Alaska even found a way to convert the settlement of aboriginal claims and parkland designations to find prosperity from Native corporations and expanded tourism. At the same time, in a century of American ownership the governmental presence changed from benign neglect to breathtaking subsidy.

History abounds in surprises, but continued growth seems inevitable because of national population pressures, technological advances and world demand for oil, natural gas, minerals, fish and timber. Alaska has overcome the difficulties of environment and distance, and Anchorage is now viewed as one of the world's most prosperous northern cities. Alaskans once complained that outside interests in New York, Washington, D.C. and Seattle wielded too much influence. But after statehood bureaucrats in Juneau and Anchorage came to exercise considerable power and now more than one in five Alaska workers are government employees within the state.

Alaska is still a place for pioneers, like Stevens, Hammond, Hickel, Rasmuson and Palin, who represent the best of Alaska's recent past. Alaskans now look to the future with new leaders and a sense of their history as the state addresses the trials of the 21st century. Just as leaders did decades ago when the trans-Alaska pipeline system jump-started the oil economy, Alaskans will be challenged to reinvent themselves to overcome the risks of isolation and have their rich and varied resource potential work for them.

Alaskans can pursue economic development on their own terms because the state and Native corporations own much of its resource base. Enlargement of the oil industry remains the best option today. Oil has been good to Alaska, as the petroleum industry contributes more than 80 percent of the State of Alaska's revenues and supports about a third of the state's work force. Since the pipeline began pumping in 1977, average personal income has risen fivefold. There is still no income or state sales tax, and every October each resident receives an Alaska Permanent Fund dividend check.

Oil production from Prudhoe Bay and its outlying fields continues to decline, so new resources are essential. Existing fields must be reexamined for further capability, such as "heavy oil" at Prudhoe Bay, while others continue to pursue opening the "1002 area" of the Arctic National Wildlife Refuge. This is still a polarizing national issue. Alaskan residents, trade unions and business interests have supported drilling in the refuge, but environmental groups and many Americans have traditionally opposed it. Senator Stevens was frustrated this was the one issue that eluded his grasp.

There are oil prospects in sensitive offshore areas, like the Beaufort Sea and Chukchi Sea, but Native communities and environmentalists have resisted exploratory drilling. These debates underscore the fact that residents are questioning the consequences of energy extraction, despite considerable past successes, and perhaps recognize the modern limits of the pioneer spirit that built the state.

Other Alaskans follow Walter Hickel's encouragement and believe Alaska's economic future is bound to a natural gas pipeline, perhaps an All-Alaska route. But unstable world markets and uncertain realities of the North Slope reserves make natural gas a questionable prospect. After decades of debate Governor Sarah Palin convinced the state legislature to jump start a 3,600 mile pipeline to carry natural gas from the North Slope to Canadian and Midwest markets. Because the project would follow the existing oil pipeline and highways, it has not raised significant opposition. But considerable work remains, as new Alaska leaders must rise to the challenge to guarantee development.

Another major economic engine has been the Congressional appropriation process. While Senator Stevens served on the Senate Appropriations committee, Alaska achieved considerable power. Although sometimes ridiculed for unnecessary bridge developments, it is clear one person's embarrassing earmark is another's essential project. But with the loss of Senator Stevens and growing federal deficits, such federal appropriations may diminish over time.

Alaska's economic expansion has depended in large part on the success of Native corporations. The Alaska Native Claims Settlement Act created these corporations so they could stand on their own and empower their shareholders with participation in the state and national economy by doing business, generating jobs, earning profits and distributing dividends. Participation in the 8(a) program has helped these companies diversify and transform Alaska's economy. Today these corporations recognize the 8(a) program may be reshaped to benefit the Nation and its treasury.

The state's other natural resource sectors are not large enough to support the economy in the way oil and federal dollars and programs have. Mining has been an essential part of the Alaska economic landscape. While Red Dog, Greens Creek, Usibelli, Pogo and Fort Knox mines continue to generate substantial wealth, the Pebble prospect, near the headwaters of valuable salmon streams flowing into Bristol Bay, is divisive. Mineral companies are determined to open the mine despite opposition from Native Alaskans, environmentalists and supporters of the local fisheries.

Alaska's fisheries are some of the richest in the world, with fishermen harvesting hundreds of millions of dollars' worth of salmon, crab, herring, halibut, pollock and groundfish every year. The exploitation and poor fisheries management took a heavy toll on the industry, but drastic measures adopted after statehood saved the industry. Today Alaska establishes necessary regulations in fisheries management as scientists determine catch levels and the location of "no-fishing zones" to protect the resource and competing species. As a result these fisheries are among the most lucrative in the world and, despite recent population fluctuations attributable to climate change, the harvestable biomass is large and should sustain itself in perpetuity.

The challenge of Alaska tourism is the appropriate balance between cruise ship and independent tourism. After the Alaska National Interest Lands Conservation Act, tourism in all sectors jumped as people from outside the state recognized the unmatched lure of the Great Land. Glacier Bay and other coastal destinations are the main attractions, but more than half of Denali National Park's visitors are cruise ship vacationers who arrive at the park by train and tour the park by bus. But the cruise ship industry is sensitive to international trends and local perceptions, particularly after Alaskans imposed new taxes and the industry considered different destinations. While this relationship is on the road to recovery, it is important that Alaska attract independent tourists, summer backcountry and recreational fishermen and hunters, as well as winter tourists to its ski resorts and dog sled championships. The 50th Anniversary of Alaska statehood was commemorated on a postage stamp with an image of a dog sled team. Iditarod and backcountry mushing have come to symbolize the Alaska sourdough and independent tourism.

The future of Alaska is not simply a recitation of its economic potential, but also how it can pay for the local government it has come to enjoy. When Governor Hammond set oil revenues aside in the Alaska savings account there was an assumption it would be used for a "rainy day." But since it was created, large surpluses have accumulated while the state general fund has struggled. The ultimate uses of the Permanent Fund were not spelled out at its inception, so there is no consensus over what role its earnings should play in the future. Some people argue that the original intent was to fund state government after the temporary oil riches ceased. But in 1999, when oil prices dropped to $9 per barrel, Alaskans voted that earnings should not be used for government purposes. This suggests Alaskans think of it as a "permanent dividend fund." Legislators willing to suggest spending the Permanent Fund's annual earnings do so at their peril.

While the Native heritage defines Alaska, today a broad mixture of international cultures exist. In Anchorage, for example, students come from homes that speak nearly 100 different languages. By necessity Alaskan leaders should expand their perspectives and continue to invest in these bountiful human assets. There has always been broad support for public education to teach people of all backgrounds and cultures, both at the local and university level. The reputation and success of local schools and the University of Alaska merits this continuing investment. A well-educated work force will generate the private-sector jobs and the public-sector tax base that will bring Alaska prosperity in future decades.

Yentna Glacier, 1966, Denali National Park and Preserve. Courtesy of National Park Service, Anchorage.

The most unpredictable issue facing Alaska is global warming. Alaskans are watching climate change from a closer vantage point than most Americans, as eroding villages, shrinking glaciers and massive forest fires impact daily life from North Slope villages to suburban Anchorage. The damage will apparently only get worse, as thawing permafrost and rising waters could add billions to infrastructure costs in a few decades. While a hard political pill to swallow, leaders will continue to be challenged by climate change and, despite the impacts to our oil-dependent economy, their commitment to greenhouse gas reduction.

Appendices

1
40 Movies and TV series filmed in or about Alaska

1924—The Chechahcos. Prospectors struggle against the elements and themselves in silent era film with Alaskan backdrop, including majestic glaciers and gold fields. Filmed entirely in Alaska, the only film ever made by the Alaska Moving Picture Corp.

1932—Eskimo. Major MGM feature starring Alaskan Ray Mala, portrayed as a happy Eskimo living in natural bliss until his life is disastrously changed when he meets up with an unscrupulous white trader. It won the first Oscar for Best Film Editing at the Academy Awards and is well regarded for preserving Inupiat culture and language on film. Filmed near Teller, Alaska.

1935—The Call of the Wild. Clark Gable and Loretta Young in Jack London classic about gold mining, dog mushing and love in the Yukon. Filmed in California and Washington State.

1938—Spawn of the North. Friends since childhood, Henry Fonda and George Raft are on opposite sides in a salmon fishing conflict. The movie won an Oscar for cinematography, presumably because of some great location shooting, including fishing boats and the waterfront in Ketchikan.

1942—The Spoilers. Based on a Rex Beach novel starring Randolph Scott, Marlene Dietrich and John Wayne. Thin plot with Nome gold miners fighting to save their claims from a corrupt mine commissioner. Based on a crude 1914 silent movie version with the same title. Filmed in Yukon Territory, Canada.

1946—Road to Utopia. A Bob Hope, Bing Crosby, Dorothy Lamour "road" movie, where Hope and Crosby are two vaudeville performers who go to Alaska to make their fortune. The screwball plot centers on a chase to find a map to a secret gold mine, with plenty of songs, pratfalls and sight gags following the Hope-Crosby formula. Filmed in California.

1952—The World in his Arms. Adapted from a Rex Beach novel, Gregory Peck is a seal poacher in Russian Alaska who woos a Russian countess in 1850 San Francisco, played by Ann Blyth. Later they are involved in a dangerous race to the Pribilof Islands. Also stars Anthony Quinn as Peck's nemesis. Peck and Blyth at the prow of the vessel foreshadows the famous Di Caprio/Winslet scene at the helm of Titanic. Studio film with Alaska background sequences, including seal hunting scenes.

1952—Lost in Alaska. Abbott and Costello star as two volunteer firemen who rescue a suicidal gold prospector, only to find he's wanted back home in the Alaskan gold fields. Not regarded as one of their best, but still a raucous comedy with very little to do with Alaska.

1960—North to Alaska. John Wayne is a macho gold miner in an improbable slapstick story about love and life during the Nome gold rush. Filmed entirely in California; the town of Nome is briefly pictured in the era of the 1900 Gold Rush.

1960—Ice Palace. Adapted from the Edna Ferber novel that advocated Alaska statehood, Richard Burton is a canner and Robert Ryan a fishing boat captain, who together establish a fish cannery in Alaska. Through the years they find themselves on opposite sides of Alaska's bid for statehood. Partially filmed in Petersburg, Southeast Alaska.

1983—Never Cry Wolf. Disney movie of Farley Mowat book starring Charles Martin Smith and Brian Dennehy. Smith is a northern wolf biologist who is asked to gather information about the savagery of wolves, only to learn the many positive attributes of the species. He tries to take on wolf attributes as he studies a courageous wolf pack of skillful providers and devoted protectors of their young. Partially shot near Nome, as well as the Yukon Territory and British Columbia, Canada.

1985—Runaway Train. Jon Voight and Eric Roberts are escaped convicts and Rebecca De Mornay is a railway worker trapped on a train with no brakes. Filmed in part on the Alaska Railroad during winter near Girdwood and Whittier.

1990—The Hunt for Red October. A new, technologically superior Soviet sub, the Red October, is heading for the U.S. coast. Stars Sean Connery, Alec Baldwin, Scott Glenn and Sam Neill. Opening sequence filmed in Valdez.

1990—Northern Exposure. Popular six-year CBS television series that won many Emmy Awards. The show was set in the fictional town of Cicely, Alaska, with humorous and poignant stories on the cultural clash between a transplanted New York doctor and the local townspeople. Actually filmed in Roslyn, Washington.

1991—White Fang. Jack London's adventure about the friendship between a Yukon gold hunter and a mixed dog-wolf, starring Ethan Hawke. Filmed in and around Haines.

1991—Salmonberries. K. D. Lang is a woman from small town Alaska who befriends a librarian, an East German immigrant who lost her husband while escaping from behind the Iron Curtain. Partially filmed in Kotzebue.

1992—Leaving Normal. A female buddy picture chronicling the hardships of two young women on a cross-country adventure as one is on her way to claim homestead land in "Palmer Valley, Alaska." They never get to Alaska. Filmed in British Columbia, Canada.

1994—On Deadly Ground. Steven Seagal and Michael Caine battle to save Alaska wilderness and Alaskans from rapacious oil companies and similar ilk, based loosely on Exxon's reputation after the oil spill in Prince William Sound. Filmed in part at the Worthington Glacier near Valdez.

1996—Alaska. A former airline pilot crashes in Alaska's mountains. Annoyed that the authorities are not doing enough to find their father, his children set out to find him with the help of a polar bear saved from a ferocious poacher, played by Charleton Heston. The movie stars Thora Birch, Vincent Kartheiser, and Charlton Heston. Heston's son, Fraser Clarke Heston, directed the film, which starred Kartheiser before he went on to success as Pete Campbell in "Mad Men." Filmed in British Columbia, Canada.

1997—The Edge. Anthony Hopkins and Alec Baldwin star as a billionaire and his pilot who survive in the woods after their small plane crashes near a lake in remote Alaska wilderness. Elle MacPherson is Hopkins' wife, but she is Baldwin's love interest, assuring considerable melodrama. Filmed in Alberta and British Columbia, Canada.

1999—Limbo. John Sayles film starring David Strathairn, Mary Elizabeth Mastrantonio and Kris Kristofferson about a small town in Alaska. Filmed in Juneau.

1999—Mystery, Alaska. Russell Crowe stars in a comedy about residents of a small Alaska town that must put aside their petty differences when their local hockey team meets the New York Rangers in a nationally televised event. Filmed in Alberta, Canada.

1999—Avalanche/Escape from Alaska. After losing her husband in an avalanche, a woman challenges a greedy corporation that improbably wants to extend an oil pipeline across the tundra above Juneau. Filmed near Palmer.

2001—Chilly Dogs/Kevin of the North. A Leslie Nielsen comedy about a Los Angles salesman who is forced to participate as a dog musher in the Iditarod sled dog race as a condition of his inheritance from his legendary grandfather. Filmed mostly in British Columbia, Canada, but with a finish line scene shot in Nome.

2001—The Barber. Malcolm McDowell is a local barber and serial killer in small town Alaska. The geographic location features 24 hour darkness, which supports the psychological darkness that drives McDowell to go on a murderous rampage. Filmed in British Columbia, Canada.

2001—Out Cold. Comedy about snowboarders living at Bull Mountain, Alaska, a no frills ski resort. The owner dies and his son decides to sell the mountain to a sleazy land developer. Stock footage from Denali National Park. Otherwise, filmed in British Columbia, Canada.

2002—Snow Dogs. Cuba Gooding Jr. is a Miami dentist who travels to Alaska to collect his inheritance, a pack of rowdy sled dogs. He learns how to run the dogs and takes part in the "Arctic Challenge" sled dog race. Filmed in Alberta and British Columbia, Canada.

2002—*Insomnia.* Psychological thriller starring Al Pacino and Robin Williams. Filmed in part in Valdez and Hyder.

2004—*50 First Dates.* Adam Sandler and Drew Barrymore learn to love despite Barrymore's daily short-term memory loss. Although filmed mostly in Hawaii, the last scene is on Sandler's sailboat amongst glaciers in Blackstone Bay, Prince William Sound near Whittier.

2005—*Grizzly Man.* Documentary directed by Werner Herzog chronicling the life and death of a rather peculiar bear enthusiast, Timothy Treadwell, who lived with brown bears in Southwest Alaska.

2005—*Deadliest Catch: Crab Fishing in Alaska.* Discovery Channel documentary series chronicling the real-life high seas adventures of Alaska crab fishermen. Filmed in the Bering Sea and other locations in the waters off Alaska.

2006—*The Guardian.* Kevin Costner and Ashton Kutcher star as US Coast Guard School swimmers. The opening story is loosely based on a 1981 helicopter disaster when a Kodiak-based Coast Guard crew crashed into Prince William Sound while attempting to hoist the survivors of a boat in distress. Partially filmed in Kodiak.

2006—*Men in Trees.* A short-lived television series starring Anne Heche as an advice columnist who travels to Alaska on a book tour and decides to stay in a remote town after finding out her fiancé cheated on her. The ratio of men to women is ten to one, so she decides she can truly learn how to find and keep a good man in Alaska. Filmed in Vancouver, British Columbia.

2007—*The Simpsons Movie.* Based on the popular animated television series. In the movie the family flees their home in Springfield for a new start in Alaska, only to return and ultimately save the day. While briefly in Alaska, the writers poke fun at all things Alaska. In one gag, without asking, Homer Simpson is handed $1,000 cash by the border guard when he enters Alaska, a jibe at the Alaska Permanent Fund.

2007—*30 Days of Night.* Horror feature set in Barrow, but filmed in New Zealand.

2007—*Into The Wild.* Sean Penn directed the Jon Krakauer book following the bizarre adventures of Christopher Mc-

Candless, who died in a remote abandoned bus in Alaska in 1992. Filmed and set in Alaska near Denali National Park.

2007—Ice Road Truckers. History Channel documentary about adrenaline-pumping truck driving on dangerous Arctic ice roads. Filmed at Prudhoe Bay, Alaska and the Northwest Territories, Canada.

2008—Snow Buddies. One of many of Disney's straight-to-video "Air Bud" movies featuring talking puppies. This time they venture to the frosty arctic and team up with new friends in a dogsled race across Alaska. Filmed in British Columbia, Canada.

2009—The Proposal. Sandra Bullock is a Canadian citizen who forces her assistant, Ryan Reynolds, to marry her so she can remain in the United States. They fly to Sitka to inform his family about their impending marriage, including his grandmother, played by Betty White. Alaska scenes are all filmed in Massachusetts.

2012—Everybody Loves Whales. A romantic comedy starring Drew Barrymore about the true story of three California gray whales trapped in the ice near Barrow. The film also stars John Krasinski from "The Office" and Ted Danson from "Cheers." This is the first big budget Hollywood movie shot completely in Alaska complete with local traffic snarls, celebrity sightings and walk-on actors. Even the scenes depicting places in California were shot in Alaska. Lured by tax incentives the $30 million movie is a significant milestone for Alaska movie making after all those features about Alaska filmed in Canada and the Lower 48 states.

BONUS:

1995—Waterworld. In a future where the polar ice caps have melted and most of Earth is underwater, a mutated mariner helps a woman and a young girl find dry land. Alaska is not involved except for the cameo role of Dennis Hopper as the leader of a sea-borne gang of thugs who sail the world on the vessel *Exxon Valdez,* complete with a photo of "Saint Joe" Hazelwood, the 1989 captain of the ill-fated oil tanker that famously grounded on Bligh Reef.

2
State Symbols

State Flag: The blue field is for the sky and the forget-me-not, the state flower. The North Star is for the future of the State of Alaska, the most northerly of the Union. The dipper is for the Great Bear, symbolizing strength. Designed by John Ben "Benny" Benson, Jr., age 13, who was from Chignik but designed the flag while at the Jesse Lee Children's Home in Seward.

State Motto: North to the Future.

Nicknames: "The Last Frontier" or "Land of the Midnight Sun" or "Seward's Icebox."

State bird: Willow Ptarmigan, adopted by the Territorial Legislature in 1955. The Willow Ptarmigan is a small Arctic grouse that lives among willows and on open tundra and muskeg. Its plumage is brown in the summer, but changes to white in winter.

State fish: King salmon, adopted 1962.

State flower: Forget-Me-Not, adopted by the Territorial Legislature in 1917. This wildflower is a perennial found throughout Alaska, from Ketchikan to the Arctic Coast, and west to the Aleutians.

State fossil: Woolly Mammoth, adopted 1986.

State gem: Jade, adopted 1968.

State insect: Four-spot skimmer dragonfly, adopted 1995.

State land mammal: Moose, adopted 1998.

State marine mammal: Bowhead whale, adopted 1983.

State mineral: Gold, adopted 1968.

State sport: Dog Mushing, adopted 1972.

State tree: Sitka spruce, adopted 1962.

State dog: Alaskan Malamute, adopted 2010.

State Seal: The state seal was originally designed in 1910 while Alaska was a territory and not a state. The rays above the mountains represent the northern lights. The smelter symbolizes mining. The train stands for Alaska's railroads, and ships denote transportation by sea. The trees symbolize Alaska's wealth of forests, and the farmer, his horse, and the three shocks of wheat represent Alaskan agriculture. The fish and the seals signify the importance of fishing and wildlife to Alaska's economy.

State song: "Alaska's Flag"

> *Eight stars of gold on a field of blue —*
> *Alaska's flag. May it mean to you*
> *The blue of the sea, the evening sky,*
> *The mountain lakes, and the flowers nearby;*
> *The gold of the early sourdough's dreams,*
> *The precious gold of the hills and streams;*
> *The brilliant stars in the northern sky,*
> *The "Bear," the "Dipper," and, shining high,*
> *The great North Star with its steady light,*
> *O'er land and sea a beacon bright.*
> *Alaska's flag — to Alaskans dear,*
> *The simple flag of a last frontier.*

Alaska's official flag is based on Benny Benson's design, which was the successful entry in a territory-wide contest for schoolchildren sponsored by the American Legion in 1926. Benson was a thirteen-year-old seventh-grader living at the Jesse Lee Home in Seward. His prize was $1,000. The Alaska Territorial Legislature officially adopted his design on May 2, 1927.

In 1935 Marie Drake, Territorial Assistant Commissioner of Education, wrote a poem after reading Benson's narrative. First published in the Territory's School Bulletin, which Drake wrote and published, it became the basis for the state song.

After seeing the poem, Eleanor Dusenbury was inspired to write a song around the poem and the flag. The wife of the Commanding Officer of the Chilkoot Barracks in Haines from 1933-36, she wrote the music after she and her husband left Alaska. She said, "I wrote the music for Marie's beautiful poetry from pure unadulterated homesickness for Alaska! I shed more tears on the boat going out than I ever have before or since. I had a book on Alaska with the picture of the flag and Marie's poem."

The song became an instant success, first played unofficially in Juneau, the Territorial capital, then steadily growing in popularity over the next two decades. The Territorial Legislature adopted the song in 1955 and it became the official State song when Alaska was admitted as the 49th state in 1959.

3
Famous Alaskans
(people with international standing who were either born in Alaska or spent a considerable time in the state)

Irene Bedard, Anchorage, actress, voice of Disney's Pocahontas and starred in the film "Smoke Signals."

Tom Bodett, Homer, author, voice actor and radio personality.

Carlos Boozer, Juneau, professional basketball player with Chicago Bulls in 2011.

Mario Chalmers, Anchorage, professional basketball player with Miami Heat in 2011.

Matt Carle, Anchorage, professional ice hockey player with Philadelphia Flyers in 2011.

Chad Carpenter, Wasilla and Anchorage, cartoonist and creator of the comic strip **TUNDRA**.

Daryn Colledge, Fairbanks, professional football player with Green Bay Packers in 2011.

Ty Conklin, Anchorage, professional ice hockey player with St. Louis Blues in 2011.

Brandon Dubinsky, Anchorage, professional ice hockey player with New York Rangers.

Erik Ellington, Anchorage, professional skateboarder.

Rosey Fletcher, Anchorage and Girdwood, World Cup and Olympic snowboarder, who won the bronze medal at the Turin, Italy Winter Olympics in 2006.

Scott Gomez, Anchorage, professional ice hockey player and 2000 NHL Rookie of the Year, with Montreal Canadiens in 2011.

Kelsey Griffin, Eagle River, women's professional basketball player with Connecticut Sun in 2011.

Travis Hall, Kenai, professional football player with San Francisco 49ers in 2011.

Jewel (Kilcher), Homer, singer/songwriter, actress, poet and Grammy nominee.

Trajan Langdon, Anchorage, professional basketball player, Cleveland Cavaliers and CSKA Moscow in 2011.

Hilary Lindh, Juneau, alpine ski racer and Olympian.

Tommy Moe, Palmer and Girdwood, alpine ski racer and Olympian who won a gold downhill skiing medal at the 1994 Winter Olympics at Lillehammer, Norway.

Sarah Palin, Wasilla, former Alaska Governor and 2008 Republican vice presidential nominee.

Virgil F. Partch, born on St. Paul Island, Disney cartoonist noted for syndicated comic strip *Big George.*

Mark Schlereth, Anchorage, Super Bowl champion with Denver Broncos and television sports analyst with ESPN.

Curt Schilling, retired Anchorage Hall of Fame professional baseball player with Boston Red Sox.

Don Simpson, attended West High School in Anchorage, noted film producer of films like *Flashdance, Beverly Hills Cop, Top Gun* and *The Rock.*

Molly Smith, prominent theater director who founded Perseverance Theater in Douglas, Alaska.

Nate Thompson, Anchorage, professional ice hockey player with Tampa Bay Lightning in 2011.

4
Population and size of state; population of major communities

Alaska Census Population

1880:	33,426	1950:	128,643
1890:	32,052	1960:	226,167
1900:	63,592	1970:	300,382
1910:	64,356	1980:	401,851
1920:	55,036	1990:	550,043
1930:	59,278	2000:	626,932
1940:	72,524	2010 estimate:	710,231

Alaska has 0.22% of the Nation's population and in 2010 was the 47th most populous state, ranking ahead of Wyoming, North Dakota and Vermont.

Alaska is a large state, one fifth the size of all the other states together, reaching so far to the west that the International Date Line had to be adjusted to keep all the state in the same day. It is also the only U.S. state extending into the Eastern Hemisphere.

It is the largest state in size with 656,425 square miles, more than twice the size of Texas, which accounts for 268,600 square miles. Alaska is more than three times the size of California, the third largest state in land area. Metropolitan Anchorage is about 2,000 square miles, the size of the State of Delaware and almost twice the size of the State of Rhode Island.

Cities of 100,000 or more people

- Anchorage (only New York has a higher percentage of residents who live in the state's largest city.)

Towns of 10,000–100,000 people
- Fairbanks
- Juneau (State Capital)
- Wasilla

Towns of 1,000–10,000 people

Ketchikan	Valdez	Dillingham
Sitka	Soldotna	Cordova
Kenai	Homer	Haines
Kodiak	Nome	North Pole
Palmer	Petersburg	Hooper Bay
Bethel	Wrangell	Craig
Barrow	Kotzebue	Houston
Unalaska	Seward	Metlakatla

5
50 Books About Alaska

Barnett, James K., *Captain Cook in Alaska and the North Pacific*. Anchorage: Todd Communications, 2008.

Berton, Pierre, *Klondike: The Last Great Gold Rush, 1896-1899*. New York: Alfred A. Knopf, 1958.

Black, Lydia, *Russians in Alaska: 1732-1867*. Fairbanks: University of Alaska Press, 2004.

Bockstoce, John R., *Furs and Frontiers in the Far North: The Contest among Native and Foreign Nations for the Bering Strait Fur Trade*. New Haven: Yale University Press, 2009.

Brower, Charles D., Philip J. Farrelly and Lyman Anson, *Fifty Years Below Zero: A Lifetime of Adventure in the Far North*. Fairbanks: University of Alaska Press, 1994.

Chandonnet, Fern, *Alaska at War, 1941-1945: The Forgotten War Remembered*. Fairbanks: University of Alaska Press, 2007.

Coates, Ken, *Sinking of the Princess Sophia: Taking the North Down with Her*. Fairbanks: University of Alaska Press, 1991.

Cole, Dermot, *North to the Future: The Alaska Story 1959-2009*. Kenmore, WA: Epicenter Press, 1997.

Crittenden, Katharine Carson, *Get Mears! Frederick Mears: Builder of the Alaska Railroad*. Portland, OR: Binford & Mort, 2002.

Crowell, Aaron A. (editor), Rosita Worl (editor), Paul C. Ongtooguk (editor) and Dawn T. Biddison (editor), *Living Our Cultures, Sharing Our Heritage: The First Peoples of Alaska*. Washington: Smithsonian Institution Press, 2010.

Davidson, Art, *Minus 148 Degrees: The First Winter Ascent of Mount McKinley*. Seattle: Mountaineers Books, 1999.

Davidson, Art, *In the Wake of the Exxon Valdez*. San Francisco: Sierra Club Books, 1990.

Day, Beth, *Glacier Pilot: The story of Bob Reeve and the Flyers who pushed back Alaska's Air Frontiers*. New York: Holt, Rinehart and Winston, 1957.

Feinup-Riordan, Ann, *Yuungnaqpiallerput/ The Way We Genuinely Live: Masterworks of Yup'ik Science and Survival*. Seattle: University of Washington Press, 2007.

Fitzhugh, William W. (editor), *Cultures in Contact; The Impact of European Contacts on Native American Cultural Institutions, A.D. 1000-1800*. Washington: Smithsonian Institution Press, 1985.

Ford, Corey, *Where the Sea Breaks Its Back: The Epic Story of Early Naturalist Georg Steller and the Russian Exploration of Alaska*. Portland, OR: Graphic Arts Center Publishing Company, 2003.

Garfield, Brian, *The Thousand-Mile War: World War II in Alaska and the Aleutians*. Fairbanks: University of Alaska Press, 1995.

Greiner, James, *Wager with the Wind: The Don Sheldon Story*. New York: St. Martin's Press, 1982.

Grinnell, George, *Harriman Expedition to Alaska: Encountering the Tlingit and Eskimo in 1899*. Fairbanks: University of Alaska Press, 2007.

Hammond, Jay, *Tales of Alaska's Bush Rat Governor: The Extraordinary Autobiography of Jay Hammond, Wilderness Guide and Reluctant Politician*. Kenmore, WA: Epicenter Press, 1996.

Harriman Alaska Expedition, *Alaska*. Charleston, SC: Nabu Press, 2010.

Hawley, Charles C. and William E. Brown, *Wesley Earl Dunkle: Alaska's Flying Miner*. Fairbanks: University of Alaska Press, 2006.

Haycox, Stephen W. (editor), James K. Barnett (editor) and Caedmon Liburd (editor), *Enlightenment And Exploration In The North Pacific 1741-1805*. Anchorage: Cook Inlet Historical Society, 1997.

Haycox, Stephen W. and Mary Childers Mangusso (editor), *Alaska Anthology*. Seattle: University of Washington Press, 1996.

Heacox, Kim (author) and Fred Hirschmann (photography), *Bush Pilots of Alaska*. Portland, OR: Graphic Arts Center Publishing Company, 1989.

Hensley, William L. Iggiagruk, *Fifty Miles from Tomorrow: A Memoir of Alaska and the Real People*. New York: Farrar, Straus and Giroux, 2009.

Huntington, Sidney, as told to Jim Rearden, *Shadows on the Koyukuk: An Alaskan Native's Life Along the River*. Anchorage: Alaska Northwest Books, 1993.

Kimura, Gregory W., *Alaska at 50: the Past, Present and Future of Alaska Statehood*. Fairbanks: University of Alaska Press, 2009.

Langdon, Steve J., *The Native People of Alaska*. Anchorage: Greatland Graphics (4th edition), 2002.

Littlepage, Dean, *Steller's Island: Adventures of a Pioneer Naturalist in Alaska*. Seattle: The Mountaineers Books, 2006.

Marshall, Robert, *Arctic Village: A 1930s Portrait of Wiseman, Alaska*. Fairbanks: University of Alaska Press, 1933.

Miller, Orlando W., *The Frontier in Alaska and the Matanuska Colony*. New Haven: Yale University Press, 1975.

Morgan, Lael and Christine Ummel (editor), *Good Time Girls of the Alaska-Yukon Gold Rush: A Secret History of the Far North*. Kenmore, WA: Epicenter Press, 1998.

Muir, John, *Travels in Alaska*. Boston: Mariner Books, 1998.

Murie, Margaret E., *Two In the Far North*. Anchorage: Alaska Northwest Books, 1957.

Naske, Claus M., *Ernest Gruening: Alaska's Greatest Governor*. Fairbanks: University of Alaska Press, 2004.

Naske, Claus M. and Herman E. Slotnick, *Alaska: A History of the 49th State*. Norman, OK: University of Oklahoma Press (second edition), 1987.

Olson, Wallace, *Alaska Travel Journal of Archibald Menzies, 1793-1794*. Fairbanks: University of Alaska Press, 1993.

O'Neill, Dan, *The Firecracker Boys*. New York: St. Martin's Griffin, 1995.

Roderick, Jack, *Crude Dreams: A Personal History of Oil and Politics in Alaska*. Kenmore, WA: Epicenter Press, 1997.

Ross, Ken, *Pioneering Conservation in Alaska*. Denver: University Press of Colorado, 2006.

Salisbury, Gay and Laney, *The Cruelest Miles: The Heroic Story of Dogs and Men in a Race Against an Epidemic*. New York: W. W. Norton & Company, 2005.

Sherwonit, Bill, *To the Top of Denali: Climbing Adventures on North America's Highest Peak*. Anchorage: Alaska Northwest Books, 2000.

Sherwonit, Bill, *Iditarod: The Great Race to Nome*. Seattle: Sasquatch Books, 2002.

Smith, Barbara S. (editor) and Redmond J. Barnett (editor), *Russian America: the Forgotten Frontier*. Tacoma: Washington State Historical Society, 1990.

Strohmeyer, John, *Extreme Conditions: Big Oil and the Transformation of Alaska*. New York: Simon and Schuster, 1993.

Stuck, Hudson, *The Ascent of Denali*. New York: Cosimo Classics, 2007.

Whitehead, John S. S., *Completing the Union: Alaska, Hawai'i and the Battle for Statehood*. Albuquerque NM: University of New Mexico Press, 2004.

Wickersham, James, *Old Yukon: Tales, Trails, Trials*. Fairbanks: University of Alaska Press, 2009.

Woodward, Kesler E., *Sydney Laurence: Painter of the North*. Seattle: University of Washington Press, 1990.

Index